Tax Policy and Gender Equality

A STOCKTAKE OF COUNTRY APPROACHES

OECD

BETTER POLICIES FOR BETTER LIVES

This document, as well as any data and map included herein, are without prejudice to the status of or sovereignty over any territory, to the delimitation of international frontiers and boundaries and to the name of any territory, city or area.

The statistical data for Israel are supplied by and under the responsibility of the relevant Israeli authorities. The use of such data by the OECD is without prejudice to the status of the Golan Heights, East Jerusalem and Israeli settlements in the West Bank under the terms of international law.

Please cite this publication as:
OECD (2022), *Tax Policy and Gender Equality: A Stocktake of Country Approaches*, OECD Publishing, Paris, https://doi.org/10.1787/b8177aea-en.

ISBN 978-92-64-80745-7 (print)
ISBN 978-92-64-98008-2 (pdf)
ISBN 978-92-64-97115-8 (HTML)
ISBN 978-92-64-45004-2 (epub)

Revised version, March 2022
Details of revisions available at: https://www.oecd.org/about/publishing/Corrigendum-Tax-Policy-and-Gender-Equality.pdf

Foreword

This report provides an overview of how countries are considering gender equality within their tax systems, focusing on how it is incorporated into the tax policy design process, as well as key sources of implicit and explicit bias, and data available for analysis. The report also considers priorities and avenues for future work on ensuring that tax policy and tax systems more broadly contribute to governments' gender equality goals.

The report was prepared as part of the OECD's efforts to mainstream gender equality and for presentation to the G20 Finance Ministers and Central Bank Governors at their meeting to be held in February 2022. The report is primarily based on countries' responses to a questionnaire that was circulated in July 2021 by the OECD to all members of the G20/OECD Inclusive Framework on Base Erosion and Profit Shifting. Responses were received from 43 countries, including from the G20, the OECD and beyond.

The report contains three sections in addition to an executive summary and the introduction: Chapter 2 provides an overview of the key concepts of gender outcomes in the tax system, Chapter 3 explores country approaches to tax policy and gender equality, and Chapter 4 provides for conclusions and implications for policy-makers.

This report was produced by the Tax Policy and Statistics Division of the OECD's Centre for Tax Policy and Administration. It was co-ordinated by Michelle Harding and Julien Jarrige and written jointly by Zipporah Gakuu, Michelle Harding, Julien Jarrige and Eugénie Ribault, with significant contributions by Ibtissem Maouene. The authors would like to thank the delegates of Working Party No.2 on Tax Policy Analysis and Tax Statistics for their inputs. The authors would also like to thank David Bradbury and Grace Perez-Navarro for their guidance. The authors are also grateful to Willem Adema, Malo Ceillier, Erwan Cherfaoui, Karena Garnier, Hazel Healy, Natalie Lagorce, Michael Sharratt, Violet Sochay, Joseph Stead and Carrie Tyler for their comments and practical assistance.

Table of contents

FIGURES

TABLES

Follow OECD Publications on:

http://twitter.com/OECD_Pubs

http://www.facebook.com/OECDPublications

http://www.linkedin.com/groups/OECD-Publications-4645871

http://www.youtube.com/oecdilibrary

http://www.oecd.org/oecddirect/

This book has... *StatLinks*

A service that delivers Excel® files from the printed page!

Look for the *StatLinks* at the bottom of the tables or graphs in this book.
To download the matching Excel® spreadsheet, just type the link into your Internet
browser, starting with the *https://doi.org* prefix, or click on the link from the e-book
edition.

Executive summary

Promoting gender equality, as reflected in the Universal Declaration of Human Rights and the Sustainable Development Goals, is a human rights objective for many governments, including in G20 and OECD countries.

Improving gender equality is not only an issue of fairness but can also produce a significant economic dividend. Working towards more inclusive economies in which women participate fully is important for economic growth and, in the context of the COVID-19 pandemic, will be crucial in ensuring an inclusive and robust recovery. Research shows that improving gender equality and reducing gender-based discrimination can generate substantial economic benefits, by increasing the stock of human capital, making labour and product markets more competitive, and increasing productivity.

Tax policy can contribute to gender equality and to governments' efforts to reduce inequalities. A growing body of research shows that even in tax systems that do not include overt gender biases, other implicit biases exist due to the interaction of the tax system with differences in the nature and level of income earned by men and women, consumption decisions, the ownership of property and wealth, and the impact of different social expectations on male and female taxpayers.

Against this background, governments can act to improve the gender outcomes of taxation; removing overt biases and reconsidering tax settings that currently result in implicit gender bias; and evaluating avenues within the tax system to design and implement tax policy that promotes gender equality.

The first analysis of its kind

The report *Tax Policy and Gender Equality: A Stocktake of Country Approaches* is the first cross-country report to analyse national approaches to tax policy and gender outcomes, including assessments of explicit and implicit biases, tax policy reforms to improve gender equity, and policy processes and priorities. Covering 43 countries from the G20, the OECD and beyond,[1] this report has been prepared as part of the OECD's efforts to mainstream gender equality and will be presented to the G20 Finance Ministers and Central Bank Governors in February 2022.

This report focuses on various aspects of tax policy design and implementation, on a cross-country basis. It explores the extent to which countries consider gender equality in tax policy development and tax administration, how they address explicit and implicit gender biases in their tax systems, and the availability and use of gender-disaggregated data. It analyses country perspectives on how and to what extent gender should be taken into account in the tax policy development process (including via gender budgeting). It also takes stock of the impact of the COVID-19 pandemic on gender equality in the tax system and highlights how countries considered gender outcomes in their tax responses to the pandemic.

Key findings and country priorities

The report finds that gender equality is an important consideration in tax policy design for most countries, and that about half of them have already implemented specific tax reforms to improve gender equity, most commonly in the taxation of personal income.

Although few countries noted examples of explicit bias in their tax system, more than half of the countries indicated that there was a risk of implicit bias. As with explicit biases, these implicit biases can either exacerbate or reduce gender inequalities already present in society and the examples noted by countries suggest a more nuanced policy response to gender bias in taxation is needed.

Most countries have access to gender-differentiated data for policy analysis, but access to data is concentrated on male and female incomes and labour market participation. Detailed data on consumption and on property and wealth ownership is less commonly available and was identified by several countries as a key data gap.

Finally, countries indicated that aspects of labour taxation were the key priority for future work to improve tax systems to increase gender equality. Identified policy areas include the impact of tax credits and allowances on gender equality, the taxation of second earners, the relationship between the progressivity of the tax system and gender equality, and the impact of social security contributions. A secondary priority is work on identifying the policy rationales and an assessment framework for considering the use of explicit biases to reduce gender inequality. Another common priority is exploring gender bias in the taxation of capital income and capital gains, notably in wealth and inheritance taxes.

Taking the work forward

There are many implications for policymakers. A useful step for countries to further address the impact of implicit bias in their tax systems is to provide more guidance on taking gender equality into account in tax policy design and tax administration. Consideration of the impact of changes in the tax structure over time is also important to assess. In addition, the report highlights the need to improve the collection of gender-disaggregated data on taxation in general, and on men and women's consumption and property and capital ownership in particular, to facilitate deeper analysis of the impact of taxation on these issues.

Going forward, analysis of the gender equality implications of tax policy could build on the conclusions of the report, including through further investigation of the priorities identified by countries, with a view to deepening the analysis and identify best practices. This work could focus on identifying principles and best practices in tax systems to improve gender equality, including whether and to what extent the tax system itself can be used as a tool to reduce bias, when assessed against alternative policy tools. Further work could also focus on the overarching impact of labour taxation on gender inequality, with a particular focus on removing disincentives that discourage women from working, especially on a full-time basis.

Notes

[1] Argentina, Australia, Austria, Belgium, Brazil, Canada, Costa Rica, Croatia, Estonia, Finland, France, Germany, Greece, Hungary, Iceland, Indonesia, Ireland, Israel, Italy, Kenya, Latvia, Luxembourg, Mexico, Montenegro, Netherlands, New Zealand, Norway, Peru, Portugal, Romania, San Marino, Saudi Arabia, the Slovak Republic, Slovenia, South Africa, Spain, Sweden, Switzerland, Tunisia, Ukraine, United Kingdom, United States and Uruguay.

1 Overview and context

Promoting gender equity, reducing discrimination on the basis of gender, and ensuring the economic participation of women, are important human rights objectives for many governments and international organisations, as reflected in the Sustainable Development Goals,[1] the UN Declaration of Human Rights, the Treaty on European Union (TEU),[2] or the G20 Leaders' commitments – reaffirmed at their November 2021 Summit – to gender equality and women's empowerment (G20 Rome Summit, 2021[1]) The establishment of global initiatives such as UN Women[3] and Women G20[4] also reflected the need for dedicated discussions and projects aiming at improving gender equality in various policy areas. Promoting gender equality in societies –is also a priority for the OECD and is part of its Programme of Work. In October 2021, the OECD Ministerial Council Meeting, gathering Ministers of Members and partners, called for policymakers to further develop the analysis of how public policies can help achieve gender equality, including by ensuring that the OECD can "model best practices in gender mainstreaming throughout its work, including through disaggregated data collection and analysis" (OECD, 2021[2]).

Beyond international commitments and human rights, working towards more inclusive economies in which women fully participate is also important for economic growth. OECD (OECD, 2016[3]) analysis indicates that gender discrimination and inequality impedes a country's level of income, particularly in developing economies. The loss associated with gender discrimination, resulting in lowering total factor productivity and reducing the level of education and labour participation among women, was estimated by the OECD at up to USD 12 trillion, or 16% of the global GDP in 2016. Against that background, improving gender equality and reducing gender-based discrimination could yield substantial economic benefits.

As the COVID-19 crisis has worsened gender inequality (as shown for instance by research from the United Nations (UN Secretary-General, 2020[4]) and the EU Parliament (European Parliament, 2021[5]) and in relation to tax, in a recent study from Danish and Swedish academics (Lind and Gunnarsson, 2021[6])), the need to develop further analysis and policy responses is critical to ensure that beyond the objective of gender equality, women can fully participate in the economic and social recovery.

Gender equity is an integral part of tax design that supports inclusive growth. Tax policy measures can have material impacts on the participation of men and women in the economy, for instance with the impact of taxes on encouraging or discouraging labour force participation, or in its impact on entrepreneurship and investment decisions. Tax policy also has a material impact on the wellbeing of citizens, and thus on gender outcomes, via its impact on disposable incomes, consumption and wealth and thus also has an important role in affecting the wellbeing of men and women.

Against this background, this report takes stock of countries' priorities and practices in relation to tax and gender, including how they address explicit and implicit biases, to what extent they take into account gender implications in policy development and budgeting, inclusion of gender considerations in tax administration and compliance, and the availability and use of gender disaggregated data. This report, which is based on a survey completed by 43 countries,[5] provides an overview of key concepts in tax policy and gender (Chapter 2) and an analysis of the information gathered and findings observed from countries' contributions, as well as considerations for policy-makers (Chapter 3). Chapter 4 concludes and discusses the implications of the survey responses.

References

European Parliament (2021), *Understanding the impact of Covid-19 on women*, https://www.europarl.europa.eu/news/en/headlines/society/20210225STO98702/understanding-the-impact-of-covid-19-on-women-infographics (accessed on 13 May 2021). [5]

G20 Rome Summit (2021), *G20 Rome Leaders' Declaration*, 2021, https://www.g20.org/wp-content/uploads/2021/10/G20-ROME-LEADERS-DECLARATION.pdf (accessed on 17 November 2021). [1]

Lind, Y. and Å. Gunnarsson (2021), *Gender Equality, Taxation, and the COVID-19 Recovery: A Study of Sweden and Denmark*, https://papers.ssrn.com/abstract=3795117 (accessed on 13 May 2021). [6]

OECD (2021), "Meeting of the OECD Council at Ministerial Level", https://www.oecd.org/mcm/MCM-2021-Part-2-Final-Statement.EN.pdf (accessed on 25 October 2021). [2]

OECD (2016), "Does gender discrimination in social institutions matter for long-term growth? Cross-country evidence", https://www.oecd-ilibrary.org/development/does-gender-discrimination-in-social-institutions-matter-for-long-term-growth_5jm2hz8dgls6-en;jsessionid=2WF6nQ_vUNbf_Zv50FybGqkU.ip-10-240-5-141 (accessed on 27 October 2021). [3]

UN Secretary-General (2020), *Policy brief: The impact of COVID-19 on women*, https://www.unwomen.org/en/digital-library/publications/2020/04/policy-brief-the-impact-of-covid-19-on-women (accessed on 13 May 2021). [4]

Notes

[1] Two SDGs target gender equality (SDG 5 "Achieve Gender Equality and Empower All Women and Girls" at https://sdgs.un.org/goals/goal5, SDG 10 "Reduce Inequalities Within and Among Countries" at https://sdgs.un.org/goals/goal10).

[2] Incorporated among the founding principles of the European Union (EU) through the TEU (Article 2, Article 3 at https://eur-lex.europa.eu/legal-content/EN/TXT/PDF/?uri=CELEX:02016M/TXT-20200301&from=EN) and Treaty on the Functioning of the EU (Article 8, Article 10 at https://eur-lex.europa.eu/legal-content/EN/TXT/PDF/?uri=CELEX:02016E/TXT-20200301&from=EN).

[3] https://beijing20.unwomen.org/en.

[4] https://w20italia.it/pages/topics/.

[5] Argentina, Australia, Austria, Belgium, Brazil, Canada, Costa Rica, Croatia, Estonia, Finland, France, Germany, Greece, Hungary, Iceland, Indonesia, Ireland, Israel, Italy, Kenya, Latvia, Luxembourg, Mexico, Montenegro, Netherlands, New Zealand, Norway, Peru, Portugal, Romania, San Marino, Saudi Arabia, the Slovak Republic, Slovenia, South Africa, Spain, Sweden, Switzerland, Tunisia, Ukraine, United Kingdom, United States and Uruguay.

2 Gender outcomes in the tax system: Key concepts

There are a number of frameworks used in the literature in assessing the impact of taxation on gender outcomes. One of the most common of these, initially developed by (Stotsky, 1996[1]), is to differentiate between tax systems that directly differentiate tax treatments based on gender as an explicit criterion, and those that do not but which interact with societal or economic differences between men and women in such a way that the tax system has a differing impact on men and women. (Gunnarsson, Spangenberg and Schratzenstaller, 2017[2]) note that this distinction broadly corresponds to the legal concept of direct and indirect discrimination, whereby "Direct (sex) discrimination is generally defined as less favourable treatment with an explicit distinction between different sexes. Indirect discrimination refers to apparently neutral provisions, criteria or practices which (might) result in a particular disadvantage for a person of one sex compared to a person of the other sex, due to existing socioeconomic differences."

Explicit bias, most commonly related to personal income tax (PIT), occurs where the tax code provisions are legally linked to gender: for instance, the allocation of exemptions, deductions and tax preferences related to spouses, or the responsibility for filing the tax return, as described in (Stotsky, 1996[1]).

Implicit bias, by contrast, occurs even if the tax system is ostensibly neutral and does not differentiate explicitly between men and women. Rather, implicit bias arises when a gender-neutral tax system interacts with differences in underlying economic characteristics or behaviours between men and women – including income levels, labour-force participation, consumption, ownership, entrepreneurship, savings, tax morale and compliance – in ways that reinforce gender biases. (Barnett, Grown, 2004[3]) consider that gender differences in economic activity can be divided into four main groups: i) gender differences in paid employment, (ii) women's work in the unpaid care economy, (iii) gender differences in consumption expenditure, and (iv) gender differences in property rights and asset ownership.

Possible implicit biases can occur across all different tax types, including via taxes on labour, consumption, corporate and capital taxation. In addressing these implicit, or indirect, biases it is important to look beyond the apparent neutrality of the tax law to assess the impact of the law with the different socioeconomic realities of men and women (Gunnarsson, Spangenberg and Schratzenstaller, 2017[2]).

In practice, much work on analysing implicit biases has focused on aspects of the PIT. The OECD has also carried out analysis in this area, including via the *Taxing Wages* models (OECD, 2021[4])and the OECD-Tax Benefit indicators (OECD, 2021[5]), which also cover various benefits affecting work incentives in addition to tax measures. (Thomas and O'Reilly, 2016[6]) and (OECD, 2016[7]) (OECD, 2016[8]) highlight how various tax design features create greater labour participation disincentives for second earners (often women) than for primary earners or single individuals, therefore, raising gender equality concerns. More generally, the OECD has noted the importance of gender equity being embedded in tax policy design as "an integral part of an inclusive growth tax policy agenda" (Brys et al., 2016[9]) (OECD, 2017[10]).

The composition of revenue taxation across different tax types can also have an impact on gender equality, particularly on a dynamic basis. This occurs via the differing impacts of various types of taxes on equity and the economic incentives provided to different taxpayers. The progressivity of the overall tax mix can reduce the tax burden on the lowest-paid, benefiting women. By contrast, low levels of taxes on capital income or on capital, or high levels of tax on consumption, can have the opposite impact. For example, (Gunnarsson, Spangenberg and Schratzenstaller, 2017[2]) note that changes in the EU since 1995 have likely shifted the tax burden in the EU towards women, given the long-term trends observed on the reduction in progressivity of personal income and wealth taxes, the decreasing tax rates on capital and corporate income, the increasing tax burden on labour incomes particularly in the low and middle income groups, as well as the higher use of consumption taxes in the tax mix.

Tax administration and compliance aspects can also have different outcomes for men and women. Tax administration processes can be more or less accessible for either gender, can be directed at a specific gender or in practice can be used by one gender more than another. The approach to tax compliance, fraud and avoidance behaviours can have gendered impacts depending on the programmes targeted, or if the approach differs depending on the gender of the taxpayer. For example, a focus on tackling fraud in relation to childcare provisions may have a deleterious effect on women's labour market participation, relative to a focus on tackling fraud in other areas, as found in (Parlementaire Ondervragingscommissie Kinderopvangtoeslag, 2020[11]) In a number of countries, including developing ones, the levels of informality bring an additional challenge: user fees and informal taxes, often used to finance basic goods such as education, healthcare and water supply, can result in a significant financial burden on households.

References

Barnett, Grown (2004), *Gender Impacts of Government Revenue Collection: The Case of Taxation*, https://gsdrc.org/document-library/gender-impacts-of-government-revenue-collection-the-case-of-taxation/ (accessed on 26 October 2021). [3]

Brys, B. et al. (2016), *Tax Design for Inclusive Economic Growth*, https://www.oecd-ilibrary.org/taxation/tax-design-for-inclusive-economic-growth_5jlv74ggk0g7-en (accessed on 13 May 2021). [9]

Gunnarsson, Å., U. Spangenberg and M. Schratzenstaller (2017), *Gender equality and taxation in the European Union*, http://www.europarl.europa.eu/supporting-analyses (accessed on 13 May 2021). [2]

OECD (2021), *OECD tax-benefit data portal*, https://www.oecd.org/els/soc/benefits-and-wages/data/ (accessed on 6 January 2022). [5]

OECD (2021), *Taxing Wages 2021*, OECD Publishing, Paris, https://dx.doi.org/10.1787/83a87978-en. [4]

OECD (2017), *A Fiscal Approach for Inclusive Growth in G7 Countries*, https://www.oecd.org/tax/tax-policy/a-fiscal-approach-for-inclusive-growth-in-g7-countries.htm (accessed on 13 May 2021). [10]

OECD (2016), *Taxing Wages 2016*, https://www.oecd-ilibrary.org/taxation/taxing-wages-2016_tax_wages-2016-en (accessed on 21 October 2021). [7]

OECD (2016), *Taxing Wages 2016*, OECD Publishing, Paris, https://dx.doi.org/10.1787/tax_wages-2016-en. [8]

Parlementaire Ondervragingscommissie Kinderopvangtoeslag (2020), *Ongekend Onrecht*, [11]
https://www.tweedekamer.nl/sites/default/files/atoms/files/20201217_eindverslag_parlementai
re_ondervragingscommissie_kinderopvangtoeslag.pdf (accessed on 13 January 2022).

Stotsky, J. (1996), *Gender Bias in Tax Systems*, https://papers.ssrn.com/abstract=882995 [1]
(accessed on 13 May 2021).

Thomas, A. and P. O'Reilly (2016), *The Impact of Tax and Benefit Systems on the Workforce* [6]
Participation Incentives of Women, OECD Tax Working Paper, https://www.oecd-
ilibrary.org/taxation/the-impact-of-tax-and-benefit-systems-on-the-workforce-participation-
incentives-of-women_d950acfc-en (accessed on 13 May 2021).

3 Country approaches to tax policy and gender equity

This chapter provides an overview of the country responses to the OECD Tax & Gender Stocktaking Questionnaire 2021, which asked countries to provide information on their priorities for tax policy and gender equality, information on implicit and explicit bias, data available for analysis of tax policy, inclusion of gender outcomes in the tax policy design process, tax administration and compliance, and priorities for future work.

3.1. Priorities for tax policy and gender equality, and links to the SDGs

The objective of improving gender equality is an international priority, notably as the fifth sustainable development goal (SDG 5), which calls on countries to achieve gender equality. Tax policy can be a tool to contribute to this objective, with various design considerations having the potential to increase gender equality. The SDGs call for countries to ensure that development and domestic resource mobilisation efforts, including tax policy interventions, do not negatively affect desired outcomes in the area of gender equality.

This chapter provides insights on country views on the role of tax policy design in supporting gender equality and domestic resource mobilisation.

3.1.1. Gender considerations in tax policy design

Gender considerations in tax policy design is considered to be at least somewhat important in two-thirds of the countries that replied. Thirty-two out of 43 countries (74%) reported this as "important" (*from 'somewhat important' to 'very important'*) (Figure 3.1). Nine countries indicated that it was of little or no importance.

Figure 3.1. How prominent are gender considerations in tax policy design in your country?

Number of countries

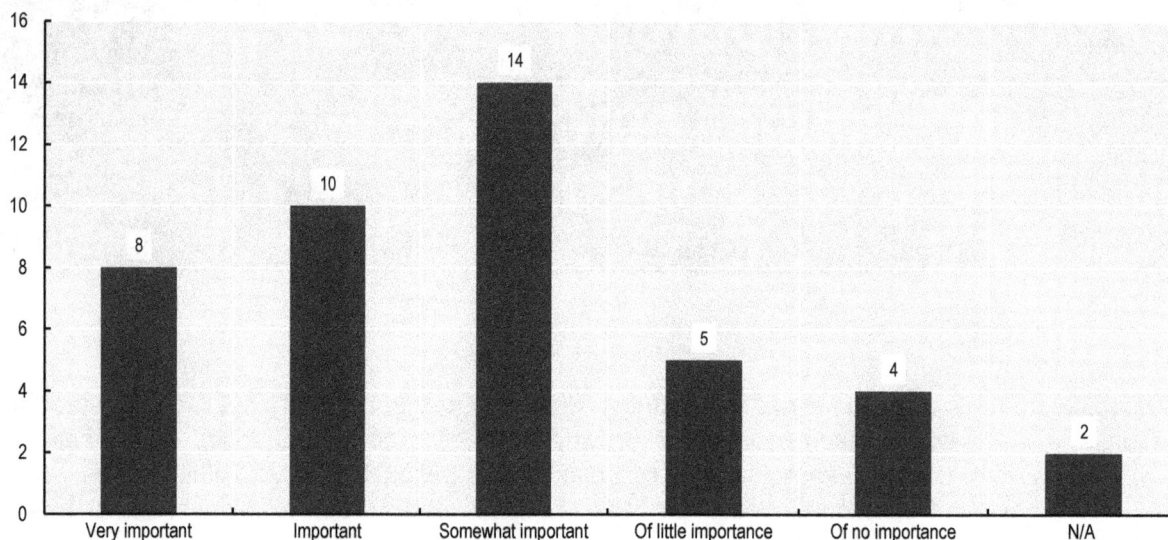

Source: OECD Tax & Gender Stocktaking Questionnaire 2021.

StatLink 🔗 https://stat.link/qhtuz1

Countries were asked whether the goal of tax policy should be to aim at gender neutrality, or to go beyond gender neutrality to consider using the tax system to compensate for existing gender distortions in society. Three-quarters of the countries that responded (32 countries or 74% of respondent countries) considered that the tax system should aim for gender neutrality. Among this group of countries, several countries indicated the importance of seeking to improve gender equality in society outside the tax system via other policy interventions, e.g. by reducing income inequalities or by social expenditure provisions (Estonia, Finland, Indonesia, New Zealand, Saudi Arabia, South Africa and Uruguay). Even when recognising that the tax system should be neutral, France noted that certain tax policy choices, including in the area of personal income taxation, could have an impact on resource allocation among individuals and therefore reduce existing distortions. The United States also noted that to the extent the tax system creates work disincentives for second earners and caregivers, the tax system should aim to reduce these distortions.

Five countries (Argentina, Austria, Belgium, Costa Rica and Kenya) indicated that the tax system should aim to reduce or compensate for existing biases. Austria and Belgium noted that this falls within broader political strategies and goals to ensure the integration of differences between men's and women's circumstances are considered in policy design. Four countries (Iceland, Portugal, Spain and Switzerland) indicated that to some degree, the tax system could pursue both gender neutrality and reducing biases. Ireland indicated that the matter was currently under review by its Equality Budgeting Expert Advisory Group and an Interdepartmental Working Group. Spain mentioned that fiscal measures should be neutral in principle, and should try to correct inequalities where there is discrimination, acknowledging the differences in opportunities and economic outcomes for men and women.

Countries were also asked to report whether or not their tax mix has an impact on gender equality. Twenty-three countries (53%) reported that their tax mix was neutral.[1] Germany and Italy noted that the primary impact of the tax system on gender outcomes was due to the design of taxes, rather than to the tax mix. Ireland noted that its Commission on Taxation and Welfare is considering the impact of the tax mix on a number of outcomes, including gender. In addition to these countries, Finland, Norway and Portugal noted that while the tax system is neutral, its interaction with elements of society may not be. In particular:

- Finland indicated that while different tax types may have differential impacts, they result primarily from differences in underlying factors, e.g. income, noting that in Finland, the share of progressive income taxes in the tax mix is high, which can be beneficial for women.

- Norway noted that the distribution of economic assets, primarily wealth, is skewed by gender, leading to potential implicit bias in that changes in the net wealth tax can affect men and women differently.

- Portugal noted that gender equality cannot be dissociated from other social goals such as combating poverty. In that regard, Portugal considers that tax measures that have improved the progressivity of general tax system (namely in what concerns the tax rate structure, personal tax credits and value-added tax (VAT) rates applied to gas and electricity) had a significant indirect impact on gender equality.

Among the 17 countries (40% of total respondents) that consider the structure of their country's tax mix affects gender equality,[2] several different types of impacts were described:

- Australia noted that their PIT system treats men and women in the same circumstances with the same taxable income consistently.

- A few countries indicated that the tax mix could contribute to reducing gender inequality, including:

  o Indonesia, which noted that gender responsive policies have been integrated into some tax regulations e.g. a married woman can now choose to obtain her own Taxpayer Identification Number, working hours for male and female staff have been adjusted to encourage equitable engagement and increase productivity, women-friendly facilities such as a lactation room, priority parking, have been implemented.

  o South Africa indicated that its tax mix is informed by their high level of income inequality, resulting in reliance on direct taxes (which constitute about two-thirds of tax revenue). The South African PIT design is highly progressive and can be seen as correcting for gender biases in the labour market.

  o The United States noted that although the structure of the tax system does not treat women and men differently, it may impact gender equality through its interaction with gender differences in income, family structure and unpaid work. For example, the progressivity of the personal income tax and the refundable earned income tax credit are beneficial for women due to the gender income gap and the prevalence of female-headed single-parent households; whereas the adoption of the household as the unit of personal income taxation and the proportionality/regressivity of the SSC rate schedule may disadvantage women.

- By contrast, several countries indicated that the impact of the tax mix could contribute to worsening gender bias:

  o Argentina indicated that VAT weighs relatively more heavily on women, who are over-represented in the lower income deciles. In Argentina, VAT and income taxes (both corporate and individual) represent more than 50% of tax revenues.

  o Estonia noted that while the exact impact of the tax mix is unclear, it is likely that the prevalence of male ownership of business and investment assets in the wealthiest income distribution group could lead to these men having a tax advantage, given that income from business ownership and investments bears a relatively lower tax burden compared to labour.

  o France indicated that tax policy can impact gender equality through labour participation, since taxation on a household basis can reduce the incentives for second earners to work – noting that in different-sex couples that are married or in civil partnerships, 78% of second earners are women (according to the French National Institute of Statistics and Economic Studies)[3] – although this impact of the tax system cannot be considered in isolation from social and family benefits and allowances applied on a household basis, as well as other policy measures such as those relating to childcare.

  o The Netherlands stated that the mix between individual and household taxes can affect the division of labour in the household.

  o The United Kingdom, stated that where women are more likely to be engaged in certain types of economic activities that are taxed differently or do not qualify for incentives, the overall impact of taxation may differ by gender, although the impact of the taxation of different sectors on women is not assessed. One example of this is that tax deductions for machinery-heavy businesses benefit men disproportionately.

- Finally, two countries noted various avenues by which the tax mix might have a differing impact by gender, also emphasising that the design of each tax is important in determining the gender impact of the tax mix:

  o Mexico noted that while VAT is regressive when analysed alone, suggesting a bias against lower-income households (where women are over-represented), other features of VAT design contain elements which could reduce this bias. Similarly, elsewhere in the tax system benefits favour low-income households, which can generate implicit biases in favour of women.

  o In Uruguay, although the design of indirect taxes is explicitly neutral in the legislation, exemptions or reduced tax rates for certain goods and services may interact with differential consumption patterns between men and women in ways that can distort the gender neutrality of the tax mix.

Twenty-two out of 43 countries (51% of respondents) indicated that tax policies or reforms have been implemented with gender equity forming one of the main rationales for the policy decision (Table 3.1). Seventeen countries indicated that reforms have not been implemented with gender equity in mind, and four countries did not respond to this question.

Table 3.1. Have any tax policies/measures or reforms been implemented with gender equity forming one of the main rationales for the policy decision

Answer	Number	Share	Countries
Yes	22	51.2%	Argentina; Belgium; Estonia; France, Iceland; Indonesia; Ireland; Israel; Italy; Kenya; Luxembourg; Mexico; Netherlands; Norway; Saudi Arabia; South Africa; Spain; Sweden; Switzerland; Ukraine; Uruguay; United States
No	17	40.5%	Australia; Austria; Brazil; Canada; Costa Rica; Croatia; Finland; Germany; Greece, Hungary; Montenegro; New Zealand; Peru; Romania; San Marino; Tunisia; United Kingdom

Note: Four countries (9.3%) did not reply to this question.
Source: OECD Tax & Gender Stocktaking Questionnaire 2021.

Among the countries that have implemented tax reforms where gender equity was a main rationale for the reform, countries noted several examples:

- Belgium adopted a royal decree on 10 December 2017 introducing a reduced rate for feminine sanitary products. France enacted a similar measure as of 1 January 2016. Australia (from 2019), Mexico (from 1 January 2022) and South Africa also apply a zero-rate on sanitary products, which are also subject to reduced rates in Kenya (Kidwingira, Mshana, Okyere, 2011[1]) and Iceland.

- Since 2017 in France, a single, divorced or separated parent living alone with at least one dependent child has benefited from an additional half share under household-based income tax rules (for the calculation of the family quotient, the basis of the French personal income tax system).

This measure predominantly benefits women, who are overrepresented among single-parent families – France reported that in 2018, 83.2% of parents in single-parent families were women.

- In Israel, the number of tax credit points for a child under five are equal for the mother and the father. The mother of a child aged 6-17 is entitled to one tax credit point every year and to half a tax credit point in the year the child turns 18. Additionally, women can decide to postpone one credit point from the child's birth year to the following year. Women's extra credit points are a means to address their lower earnings relative to men.

- In Italy, following the "Gender Budget 2019" (Italian Ministry of Economy and Finance, 2019[2]), the 2020 budget law enacted numerous equal opportunity measures, among which the renewal of temporary or pilot initiatives such as the birth allowance ('baby bonus'), the 'nursery bonus', the women's early retirement loan, and the 'women's option' early retirement scheme.

- In Norway, under the "tax class 2" ("skatteklasse 2"), partners or registered spouses could be taxed together, which was beneficial if one of the spouses or partners had income below a certain threshold. The removal of tax class 2 in 2019 was partially motivated by the need to improve work incentives for women.

- In Saudi Arabia, the horizontal Vision 2030 plan aims to empower women and to increase their participation in the workforce. Among specific measures, a monthly allowance is paid to divorced women provided certain conditions are met, and a special transportation allowance is provided to women to help work commuting.

- Spain mentioned the Organic Law 3-2007 for promoting effective equality of women and men with regard to access to employment, professional training and promotion, working conditions and access to goods and services and their supply. Since 1971, labour income has been taxed on an individual basis in Sweden. In addition, every year a general analysis of the effects on economic equality resulting from the government's policy actions, including tax policy, is undertaken (Government of Sweden, 2020[3]).

- In the United States, several reforms have been carried out with gender-related goals in mind. These include:
  - The amendment of a deduction for dependents that was able to be claimed only by a woman, widower or a husband with an incapacitated wife, to extend it to all eligible persons regardless of gender;
  - A secondary earner deduction in force between 1981 and 1986 was designed to reduce inequality between single-earner and dual-earner married couples;
  - A child and dependent care tax credit was introduced in 1976 to improve work incentives for families with children;
  - Over the last twenty years, a range of policies have been created to reduce taxation of married couples and the marginal effective tax rates for second earners, including an expansion of the earned income tax credit;
  - Several states are considering excluding feminine hygiene products from the sales tax base.

3.1.2. Targeted Measures

In the taxation of personal income, 27 of the respondent countries (i.e. 63% of total respondents) base taxation on an individual unit. Six countries (Belgium, France, Iceland, Indonesia, Switzerland and the United States) use a household unit and nine countries allow taxpayers to choose between the individual and household unit.

Table 3.2. Does your system apply individual or household-based income taxation?

Answer	Number	Share	Countries
Individual unit	27	62.8%	Argentina; Australia; Austria; Canada; Croatia; Costa Rica; Estonia; Finland; Greece; Hungary; Israel; Italy; Kenya; Latvia; Mexico; Montenegro; New Zealand; Norway; Peru; Romania; San Marino; Slovak Republic; Slovenia; South Africa; Sweden; Tunisia; United Kingdom
Household unit	6	13.9%	Belgium; France; Iceland; Indonesia; Switzerland; United States
Optional between individual and household unit	8	18.6%	Brazil; Germany; Ireland; Luxembourg; Netherlands; Portugal; Spain; Ukraine

Note: One country (2.3%) did not reply to this question. In addition, Saudi Arabia does not have a personal income tax and is therefore not included.
Source: OECD Tax & Gender Stocktaking Questionnaire 2021.

Most countries with individual taxation indicated that this unit of taxation results in encouraging female labour supply and improves equality. For Australia, individual taxation allows the second earner to have access to the tax-free threshold, which encourages work force participation. Austria notes that various studies have indicated that household-based income taxation entails negative work incentives for second earners, whereas individual-based income taxation is more neutral for gender equality. France, Mexico and the United Kingdom also highlight the detrimental impact of household taxation on gender equity via its impact on the marginal tax rates of second-earners and consequent negative labour supply effects for women. This can result in high marginal tax rates on second earners looking to enter work or to move from part-time to full-time work (OECD, 2019[4]) (Harding, Paturot and Simon, 2022 (forthcoming)[5]). In France, the National Institute of Statistics and Economic Studies estimated that because of household taxation women face a higher marginal tax rate, by 5.9 percentage points on average, compared to what it would be if they were taxed separately – even though other measures such as family allowances can incentivise the second earner's labour participation. ((INSEE, 2019[6])) In the United States, household taxation was enacted in 1948. (LaLumia, 2008[7]) estimated that this resulted in a decline of approximately 2 percentage points in the employment rate of married women, but had no impact on the labour force participation of married men.

Many countries tax personal income on an individual basis but apply tax credits or allowances on a household basis. For example, in Hungary, PIT is based on individual income, but a few measures (e.g. family allowances) can be shared among parents (not linked to marital status). Many other countries also have family-based tax credits or allowances that can lead to higher tax rates on second earners (OECD, 2016[8]). A few countries offer tax allowances or tax deductions for spouses that are not working or that have incomes below a certain limit. These spousal provisions can also have the impact of depressing second earner labour supply by providing incentives for second earners not to work or to remain under the salary threshold (e.g. by working part-time), as highlighted in (OECD, 2019[9]) in relation to the spousal deduction in Japan.

Other countries use an individual tax basis for income taxation, but a combined base for other taxes; for example, in Norway, for net wealth tax purposes, spouses are taxed together. In Greece, spouses file a joint return but each spouse is liable for the tax payable on his or her share of the joint income. In Hungary, the tax unit is, in all cases, the separate individual. However, in exceptional cases, the household can become subject to PIT, for instance in the case of benefits in kind. In the United Kingdom, the tax unit is the individual, but certain reliefs depend on family circumstances such as a marriage allowance which allows the transfer of 10% of an individual's personal allowance to their husband, wife or civil partner. The allowance is restricted to couples where the higher earner is a basic rate taxpayer and is only beneficial if the lower earner has a tax liability below the personal allowance. The allowance has to be claimed and is given only to those who meet the eligibility criteria.

Countries that allow for some or all elements of personal taxation to apply on a household basis note that the use of household-based taxation may have other benefits for gender equality, particularly for low-income taxpayers. Iceland, which also uses a household-based system, noted that joint taxation "has been systematically reduced" to encourage labour participation of the lowest paid, usually women. The law allows single people living together to choose between individual and household taxation. It also treats single-parent households, more commonly women, in the same way as dual-income households at the same income level. The federal government is currently planning a wide-ranging tax reform that is expected to bring change to this aspect of the tax legislation. The government plans a comprehensive income tax reform for 2020 involving: 1) lower tax rates for minimum-wage earners; 2) a new indexation mechanism to strengthen stabilisation properties of income taxes; and 3) improved neutrality of the tax system with respect to gender and civil status.

Although using a household-based system, Belgium took action to reform its PIT towards a system based more on individual taxation over the period 2001-2004 (Orsini, 2005[10]). Further, in 2006 Belgium introduced a change to the dependent child regime to better accommodate separated couples, known as tax co-parenting. This provision was extended to include individuals over 18, in 2016 (Federal Public Service Finance of Belgium, 2021[11]). Belgium indicated that although several reforms have been approved to move towards greater individualisation of rights (in 1988 and 2001), there are still some provisions that are not individualised.

Several other countries allow the taxpayer to choose individual or household-based taxation depending on their circumstances. Luxembourg indicated that spouses and partners are taxed jointly on their income, although from 2018 onwards, there have been options to file separate tax returns for married couples and civil partners. Luxembourg therefore does not consider the taxpayer unit to have a direct impact on gender equality, although notes that it may provide indirect incentives for the labour participation of the second earner. Spain also allows family units to choose between individual or joint tax returns, and indicated that it considers this optionality to benefit individuals with lower incomes, thus reducing gender inequality. In Ireland, the report "Taxation, work and gender equality in Ireland" (Doorley, 2018[12]) investigated whether Ireland's move from joint filing to partial individualisation of income tax had any effect on female labour supply and caring duties. The report, explaining the importance of removing barriers to work for all those who are willing and able to work, and exploring gender differences in labour market behaviour, found that the labour force participation rate of married women increased by 5-6 percentage points in the wake of the reform, hours of work increased by two hours per week and hours of unpaid childcare decreased by approximately the same margin. The Netherlands indicated that the Dutch tax system includes elements of both household and individual taxation. In principle, the unit of taxation in the PIT is the individual; however, if two people are partners for tax purposes, they can divide most deductions and some personal income components (including income from substantial interest, savings and investments) between them.

The majority of the countries surveyed (38 out of 43 – i.e. 88%) indicated that informal taxation – defined in (Olken, 2011[13]) as "a system of local public goods finance co-ordinated by public officials but enforced socially rather than through the formal legal system" – is not common or has very little presence in their country. Four countries – Kenya and Italy (*very common*), Argentina and Ukraine (*to some degree*) – indicated that informal taxation was present, and one country did not respond. Kenya indicated that the informal sector accounts for 30% of GDP and that it is considered to worsen gender bias.

3.1.3. Impact of COVID-19

Over two-thirds of the countries surveyed (30 out of 43 – 70%) indicated that COVID-19 did not necessarily worsen the risk of gender bias in the tax system. Some of these countries (Canada, Kenya and San Marino) noted that women have been impacted more than men during the COVID-19 crisis, but that this has had no, or very little, impact on the risk of gender bias in the tax system.

Nine countries indicated that COVID-19 had worsened the risk of gender bias in the tax system (Argentina, Australia, Iceland, Indonesia, Ireland, Mexico, Norway, Spain and the United Kingdom). Among these countries:

- The COVID-19 pandemic has had a significant impact on the informal sector in Argentina. In particular, domestic services, which account for 25% of informal sector employment and 17% of employed women in Argentina, were severely affected, thus deepening the income and gender gaps (Ministerio de Economía, 2021[14]) (UNICEF and DNEIyG, 2021[15]).

- Australia noted that under the Australian PIT system, a man and a woman with the same level and nature of taxable income will pay the same amount of tax. Therefore, COVID-19 will have only affected the gender distribution of tax paid to the extent it affected the underlying distribution of income between men and women in society more broadly.

- In Iceland, the VAT refund system was reformed during the pandemic to allow temporary refunds of construction projects and car repairs, which is more likely to have benefited male-dominated sectors.

- Spain indicated that over 50% of women's employment is concentrated in four sectors (commerce, tourism, education, health and social services) that were directly impacted by the COVID-19 pandemic. In addition, the recovery of employment in Spain between the second and third quarter of 2020 was somewhat higher for men than for women, widening the gender gap. Spain also noted that unpaid care tasks increased, both in caring for children and for dependent and elderly people, also revealing gender inequalities (BBVA, 2020[16]). According to Eurostat-INE data, in Spain, 95% of women are involved in the care of their children on a daily basis, compared to 68% of men. The lack of equal responsibility means that a greater burden of childcare may be falling largely on women, hindering in most cases their labour force participation (Castellanos-Torres, Mateos and Chilet-Rosell, 2020[17]).

Eleven out of 43 countries (26% of respondents) (Argentina, Australia, Austria, Canada, Finland, Iceland, Ireland, Italy, Spain, Sweden and the United Kingdom) indicated that tax policy measures introduced in response to COVID-19 were assessed for their gender impacts.

- Argentina implemented a number of measures specifically designed to protect women, non-binary employees and other vulnerable groups in the workplace during the COVID-19 pandemic. As part of measures to promote the knowledge-based economy, a higher tax deduction was allowed for the employer SSC payments made for women, non-binary workers, those with disabilities, or long-term unemployed (80% compared to 70% for other workers; (Congress of Argentina, 2020[18])); higher deductions were introduced for the director or trustee fees of women or non-binary directors, as part of measures to introduce a gender-lens to corporate income taxation (Ministerio de Economía, 2021[19])) and an "Accompany" programme was put in place for people at risk of gender-based violence (Ministerio de Economía, 2021[20]).

- Australia's Treasury undertook a distributional analysis, including a gender analysis, of the impact of extending the LMITO (low and middle income tax offset) for the 2021-22 income year. Ireland published a study on 'The gender gap in income and the COVID-19 pandemic' (Doorley, O'Donoghue and Sologon, 2021[21]), which found that the gender gap is smaller after taxes. It notes that men's market income remains higher than women's, although they suffer slightly higher loss of employment, so men continue to pay systematically more tax than women. Prior to the pandemic, the tax-benefit system was reducing the gender income gap from 40% to 35%. However, this analysis shows that the cushioning effect of the tax and welfare systems has doubled during the pandemic.

- Austria shared its willingness to contribute to impact measures targeted on the "Gender Equality goal" in the 2020 federal budget enabling the tax system to provide positive incentives to increase the employment rate.

- In Canada, as required by the Canadian Gender Budgeting Act, all tax and resource allocation decisions must consider gender and diversity impacts. Canada has introduced a number of measures to support individuals and businesses through the COVID-19 pandemic (Government of Canada, 2020[22]).

- In Spain, an assessment on gender impact is included in all regulatory projects including the measures taken in response to COVID-19.

3.2. Explicit bias

Explicit bias occurs when tax policy or tax administration settings differ for men and women, e.g. in the legislation, regulation, or other legal standards. It can include different tax rates or thresholds for men and women, explicit tax credits or taxes applying to only one gender, and tax administration arrangements that differ by gender (e.g. different access to information for men and women).

This chapter describes country responses to questions on examples of explicit bias that apply to either gender (including measures that advantage as well as disadvantage women, or where a different treatment is prescribed by gender, whatever the treatment), both currently and on a historic basis.

3.2.1. Explicit bias in current tax systems

Very few countries (7 out of the 43 respondent countries) reported instances of explicit bias in their current tax systems (Argentina, Hungary, Ireland, Israel, South Africa, Spain and Switzerland).

Argentina, Hungary, Ireland, Israel, Spain and Switzerland reported that explicit bias exists in their PIT system (allowances, tax credits, rates or thresholds). In particular:

- In Argentina prior to the modification of the Civil Code in 2015, the assets of a married couple were attributed to the husband, with some exceptions (Article 18, Decreto 281/97 de la Administración Pública Nacional), which made women invisible as taxpayers with respect to these assets. On the other hand, Argentina also implemented measures with explicit biases to compensate for gender distortions, including to promote the inclusion of women and transgender people in the formal economy in certain regions, to implement deductions for the expenses of day-care and kindergartens for parents of children under three, and for family charges for cohabiting partners (instead of only for married couples).

- In Hungary, since 2020, mothers with four or more children receive a special PIT allowance. This allowance is available only to mothers, whereas a general family tax allowance is available for both parents.

- In Israel, the measure postponing tax credit points and offering extra credit points to women (as described in Chapter 3) is also an example of explicit bias.

- The Spanish tax system also provides for a maternity deduction for children under three years of age of up to EUR 1 200 per year for each child born or adopted in Spain under Law 35/2006 on personal income tax.

- Switzerland noted that its PIT rates include bias. In Switzerland, the subject of income taxation is the household (although only if the couple is married). Household taxation combined with a progressive rate schedule leads to poor incentives for a second earner to find employment, who is often the female partner. The Supreme Court noted in 1986 that the situation is unconstitutional; however, parliament has not yet agreed on a solution and the situation has been partially remedied by means of a second earner deduction. There remain a large number of households that are still facing a "marriage penalty" in federal income taxation. In addition, a (married) household is registered and filed under the husband's name as the head of the household, regardless of who the main earner is.

In this area of social security contributions (SSCs), few countries reported examples of explicit bias. However, in Spain self-employed workers can apply a flat rate regime under certain circumstances. This regime is established for up to 30 years for men and up to 35 years for women, so that women have a time extension of the tax advantage.[4] In addition, self-employed women have other explicit advantages such as aid for single pregnant women and for single women with a child, and 16 weeks of maternity leave – with an amount of the subsidy equivalent to 100% of the contribution base. Finally, Spain indicated that women that are victims of gender violence and who must suspend their professional activity to protect themselves can receive a 100% bonus in the "freelance fee" (Debitoor, 2021[23]). In Argentina, employer SSCs were reduced in 2020 to incentivise the hiring of women, transgender people, people with disabilities and the long-term unemployed.

South Africa reported that VAT/GST has explicit bias such as the zero-rating of sanitary products. Other countries also have preferential treatment for sanitary products. The United Kingdom announced that it will apply a zero-rate to feminine hygiene products as of 1 January 2021 (OECD, 2020[24]). In addition, Belgium's federal government adopted a royal decree on 10 December 2017 introducing a reduced rate for sanitary products. In Kenya, a tax exemption was applied to sanitary products in 2004 and in 2019 Kenya was the first country in the world to create a national Menstrual Hygiene Management policy (Ministry of Health, 2019[25]) in order to provide women, girls, men and boys with information on menstruation. Iceland also provided, for menstrual products, a reduced VAT rate of 11% relative to the standard rate of 24% (see the Priorities for tax policy and gender equality section). Similarly, from 1 January 2022 a zero rate for these products applies in Mexico to promote gender equality.

Figure 3.2. Are there any examples of explicit bias in the current tax system of your country?

Number of countries

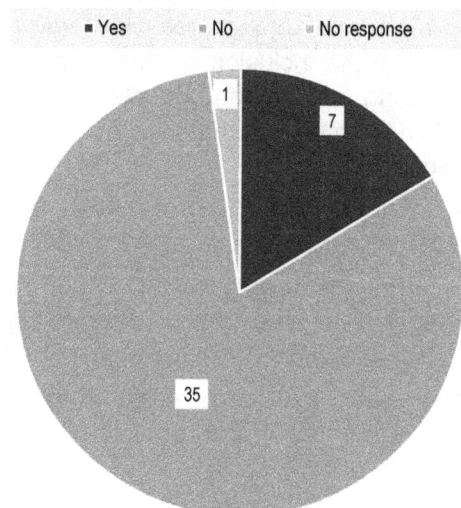

Source: OECD Tax & Gender Stocktaking Questionnaire 2021.

StatLink ⬛𝘴⃕ https://stat.link/fbax3c

3.2.2. Historic explicit bias

Three countries noted that there had been examples of explicit bias in its tax system that had since been repealed. Argentina repealed the abovementioned PIT provision, whereby marital property was attributed to the husband unless the property had been acquired by the wife prior to marriage. This gender bias was eliminated in 2017 when it was made explicit that both spouses are taxed individually on their assets and on 50% of the marital assets. Between 1980 and 1999, Ireland operated a system of income splitting, whereby married couples could reduce their tax bill by sharing allowances and rate bands between partners. In 1993, Ireland removed the requirement for this joint filing to be done in the name of the husband (Stotsky, 1996[26]). This was accompanied by other reforms to reduce implicit incentives, including the partial income tax individualisation (of the standard rate income tax bands) in 2000 with the objective to increase incentives for second earners to work and to boost female labour force participation. A final reform took place in 2002 when the standard rate bands for singles and two-earner couples were increased by 10% more than the standard rate band for one-earner couples. Whilst individualisation is beneficial to single earners, it is less favourable to single income families whose income exceeds the married one-earner tax band (currently EUR 44 300). To redress this, a tapered home careers tax credit (HCC) was introduced and has been gradually increased and extended over time.

The United States noted an explicit bias in a deduction for the expenses of the care of certain dependents in section 214 of the Internal Revenue Code. This section allowed deductions to be claimed by "a woman or widower" or "a husband whose wife is incapacited or is institutionalized". This section was amended from 1972 to allow for a broader eligibility regardless of gender.

In addition to the information provided by countries in their responses to the survey, (Stotsky, 1996[26]) noted a range of historic examples of explicit bias in the countries considered, which have since been reformed. Before 1983, in France, only the husband was required to sign a family return, whereas now both partners must do so; similarly in 1990, the United Kingdom moved from joint filing in the name of the husband to a separate assessment for both individuals. Both the Netherlands and South Africa historically imposed a higher tax burden on married women than on married men: in the Netherlands via a higher tax free allowance for married men (before 1984) and in South Africa via a higher rate schedule for single individuals and married women than for married men (reformed in 1995) (Stotsky, 1996[26]).

3.3. Implicit bias

Implicit gender bias occurs when, due to the gendered patterns of social arrangement, gender pay gaps and economic behaviour, the outcome of tax policy or administration has different implications for men than for women, and so impact on gender equity (for example in most countries the second earner in a household is likely to be female, the tax treatment of second earners may therefore impact gender equity). As with explicit bias, it can occur to the detriment of either gender.

Almost two-thirds of the countries surveyed (25 out of 43 – 58%) indicated that they have not undertaken analysis to identify and/or assess existing implicit biases in their tax system. Among those countries, four (Germany, Indonesia, Montenegro and San Marino) plan to do so in the future. In addition, the United States also noted that studies on specific topics have touched on implicit bias (e.g. studies on tax rates for second earners and the earned income tax credit, including (Department of the Treasury, U.S., 2015[27]) (Lin and Tong, 2014[28]) (Center on Budget and Policy Priorities, 2019[29])) although comprehensive examinations of implicit bias across the tax system are not available.

The limited number of countries that have assessed implicit bias may be explained by i) the fact that only half of countries consider that there is a risk of implicit bias in their tax system (23 out of 43), ii) the limited number of countries considering implicit bias questions in tax policy design (19 out of 43), iii) a general lack of guidance on how to consider or test for implicit bias in tax policy design.

The absence of guidance on how to consider or test for implicit bias in tax policy design is widespread as only five out of 43 countries surveyed reported having such a guidance (Austria, New Zealand, San Marino, Spain and Sweden). Some countries reported that they use general guidelines for assessing gender impact (Iceland), or have gender budgeting recommendations, albeit not targeted to tax policies (Ireland). In Spain, general guidance was implemented via a gender impact report in relation to the general budget, accompanied by practical implementation guidelines (Instituto de la Mujer, 2007[30]). This gender impact report has accompanied the state budgets since 2008. Since 2021, the report has been made using the "3-Rs Method" – the three "Rs" referring to "Reality", "Representation" and "Resources – Results".

Table 3.3. Is there any guidance on how to consider/test for implicit bias in tax policy design?

Answer	Number	Share	Countries
Yes	5	11.6%	Austria; New Zealand; San Marino; Spain; Sweden
No	31	72.1%	Argentina; Belgium; Brazil; Canada; Costa Rica; Croatia; Estonia; Finland; France; Hungary; Iceland; Indonesia; Iceland; Israel; Italy; Kenya; Latvia; Luxembourg; Mexico; Montenegro; Netherlands; Norway; Peru; Portugal; Romania; Slovenia; South Africa; Switzerland; Tunisia; Ukraine; United Kingdom

Note: Seven countries (16.3%) did not reply to this question.
Source: OECD Tax & Gender Stocktaking Questionnaire 2021.

Among the countries surveyed, 16 out of 43 (37%) indicated that they have undertaken analysis to identify and/or assess existing implicit bias in the tax system.[5] This analysis was either requested by a ministerial decision (six out of 16), the result of a mandatory legal requirement (four out of 16), or a departmental request (three out of 16). In Italy, this analysis followed a parliamentary request and also came from internal research. In Ireland, this analysis was undertaken at the initiative of an external research organisation, as in Uruguay where the University of the Republic initiated the analysis. In Belgium, Canada, Ireland and Italy, the request stemmed from several stakeholders.

Research into implicit bias in the tax system tends to focus on research within the personal income tax system, either due to family taxation or to the existence (or non-existence) of shared tax credits or tax allowances. For instance, in France, implicit bias risk was analysed at the request of the Parliament, leading to a 2014 report "On the Question of Women and the Tax System" (French National Assembly, 2014[31]), which examined the current tax treatment of couples, including the impacts of joint taxation and the family quotient, changes in family composition, the possibility of individualising taxation and the potential impact on women's employment and promoting tax equity and the empowerment of women. Also, following an administrative circular issued by the French Prime Minister on 23 August 2012, the impact assessments that complement each legislative bill must include an analysis of the proposed measures' impact on gender equality. Separately, personal tax credit or tax allowance (e.g. for child care), were identified as areas of risk of implicit tax biases by Argentina, who also note a risk for implicit bias given that the PIT exemption provided for financial income does not take into account the over-representation of men in the group of taxpayers reporting financial income. In the United States, although not routinely assessed, if a specific policy is expected to cause or worsen distortions, the gender impacts are considered during the policy development phase.

A few countries have also identified VAT systems as a potential source of bias, particularly in countries where VAT forms a large part of the tax base. Saudi Arabia indicated that VAT and tax treatment for micro-businesses could create similar risks, as more and more women are operating their own micro-businesses. Spain also identified VAT as an area at risk of implicit bias, together with PIT with regards to household taxation, progressivity and second income earners.

Among the 16 countries that undertook analysis to identify and/or assess existing implicit bias in their tax system, in almost half of the countries, universities or other academic institutions were involved in providing the analysis (Australia, Austria, Finland, Ireland, Italy, the Netherlands and Uruguay). In more than half of these 16 countries, the Ministry of Finance provided analysis (Argentina, Austria, Belgium, Canada, Iceland, Italy, Spain, the United Kingdom and the United States). In Austria and Italy, other government ministries were also involved in providing analysis, and in Australia and Sweden, the revenue authorities were in charge of this analysis. In France, the Parliament undertook the analysis through a parliamentary inquiry. In the United States, scholars in academia and other policy analysts also undertake research in these areas. Box 3.1 provides a typology of the sources of implicit bias noted by the 22 countries that identified possible such biases in their tax systems.

In conclusion, analysis of gender implicit bias is not widespread among the countries surveyed. Analyses about this issue seem relatively rare and most countries that have not yet undertaken this type of analysis do not plan to do so in the near future, despite their importance in raising awareness of implicit gender bias. Support from universities and academic institutions can be useful in such analyses, as they already play an important role in many countries; as well as the role of the law in requesting or considering these analyses as a factor to take into account in the policy design.

Figure 3.3. Has your country undertaken any analysis to identify and/or assess existing implicit bias in the tax system?

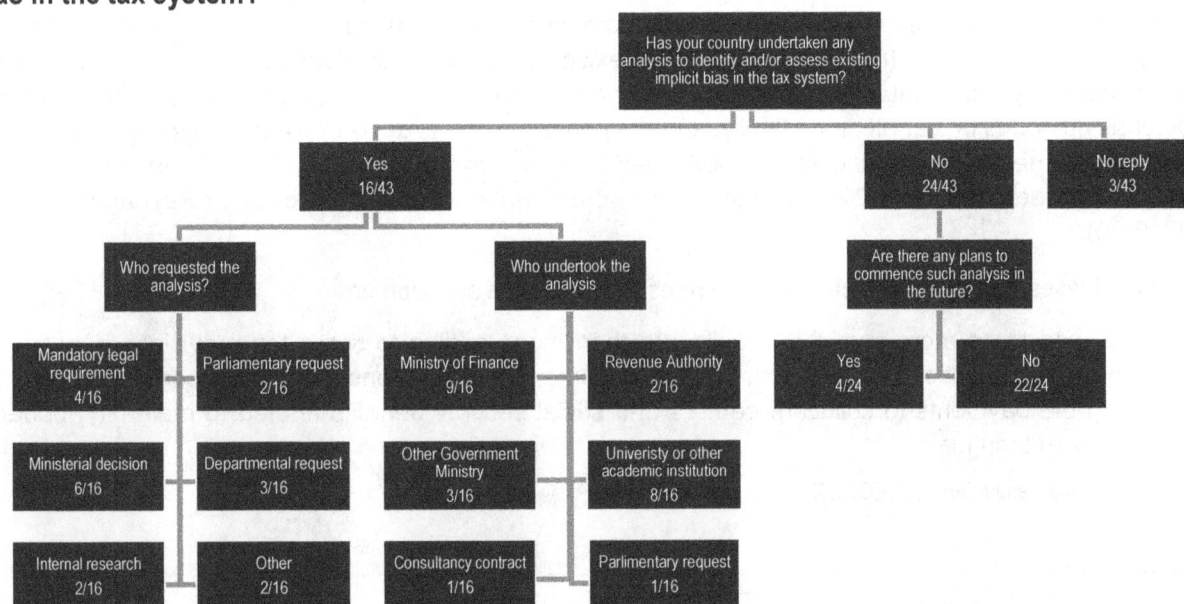

Source: OECD Tax & Gender Stocktaking Questionnaire 2021.

Box 3.1. Typology of implicit biases identified among the countries surveyed

Among the countries surveyed, 23 out of 43 (53%) identified possible implicit biases in their tax systems. This box groups these implicit biases to form a non-exhaustive typology.

Implicit biases due to differences in income levels between men and women

On average, men earn higher incomes than women. Therefore, if the PIT puts a high burden on low-income earners or is not progressive enough, there is a risk of bias in favour of men (noted by Argentina, Belgium, Finland, Ireland, Italy, Kenya, and Norway). Similarly, if VAT places a greater relative burden on individuals with low disposable income, there is risk of bias that disadvantages women (noted by Argentina, Austria and Kenya). Conversely, highly progressive tax systems, as well as refundable tax credits for lower-income earners contribute to reducing gender inequities (e.g. in the United States).

Implicit biases due to differences in nature of income between men and women

On average, men earn more capital income than women, so preferential taxation of capital can create a risk of bias in favour of men (noted by Argentina, Austria, Finland, Norway, Sweden, and the United Kingdom).

Implicit biases due to fiscal unit consideration

Taxing households rather than individuals can create implicit biases. Joint filing taxation puts a high tax burden on the second earner within a household, the second earner being more likely to be a woman. Even if joint filing is optional, risks of bias against second earners still exist (noted by Belgium, Iceland, Ireland, Italy, Kenya, Luxembourg, Spain and the United States). Belgium, Canada, Iceland, the Netherlands and Tunisia reported that even when individual filing applies, tax credits or tax allowances are often designed at the household level. Households optimise the person who will benefit from the tax relief to pay fewer taxes. These tax reliefs are often more profitable when they apply to the highest income within the household, which could be detrimental for women who earn on average less than men (the Netherlands).

Implicit biases due to differences in consumption between men and women

Essential products, such as food, medicines and educational services, often benefit from preferential taxation under VAT or excise duties, which can create a risk of bias due to the different consumption profile between genders (noted by Brazil and Mexico). However, individual consumption patterns are not necessarily representative of the gender impact of consumption taxes, as the individual may be purchasing goods on behalf of the family, and the impacts of the taxes on intra-household consumption and income decisions are unclear (as described in a Finnish study on the effects of tax changes on gender between 1993 and 2012 (Riihelä, 2015[32]) and (International Development Research Centre, 2010[33])).

Implicit biases due to differences in social roles between men and women

Women tend to be more involved in childcare than men, leading to some tax provisions benefitting women more in practice For example, in Mexico, some PIT exemptions (alimony, income received for financing the payments to childcare centres and social security benefits related to maternity) benefit women more than men.

Source: Tax and Gender Survey, OECD 2021

3.4. Policy development process and gender budgeting

Understanding and improving the gender equality of the tax system relies on policy development processes which assess the impact of taxes on gender as a core element of policy design, including through gender budgeting. This section presents information on whether and how the impact of taxes on gender fits within the tax policy process in the respondent countries. This includes the process of developing and introducing new tax policies or tax expenditures, or changes to tax rates, bases, credits, allowances, or other tax expenditures.

3.4.1. Analysis of tax and gender under the scope of gender budgeting

Sixteen out of 43 (37%) respondent countries indicated that key tax policies and programs proposed for inclusion in the budget or other legislative processes are subject to an ex-ante gender impact assessment.

Of these, six countries have had the Ministry of Finance or the budget office issuing circulars or other directives that provide specific guidance on assessing the impact of taxation on gender (Argentina, Austria, Finland, Indonesia, Italy and Sweden).

Almost 50% of respondent countries have indicated using sex-disaggregated statistics and data when available across key policies and programs to inform tax policy decisions. However, 29 out of the 43 countries indicated their government does not provide a clear statement of gender-related objectives in relation to tax policy (i.e. a gender budget statement or gender responsive budget legislation). In this regard, work is in progress in France between the Directorate General of the Treasury and the Directorate General of Social Cohesion and four ministries (Agriculture and Food, Culture, Territorial Cohesion, and Solidarity and Health) to improve a horizontal policy document on gender equality policy. They are focusing on three areas: (i) analysing the budgetary expenditures to identify the impact on equality, (ii) developing gender equality performance indicators (when relevant and where data are available) and integrating them into a budget performance model, (iii) conducting awareness-raising and training actions to take into account the equality axis in expenditure. A pilot project at the end of 2019 confirmed the objective of implementing a budget gender equality study (le Budget intégrant l'égalité (BIE)) as part of budgetary procedures and in the evaluation of expenditure performance.

Nineteen out of 43 countries surveyed (i.e. 44%) practise some form of gender budgeting, although only five countries indicated that there was a specific requirement for gender budgeting in tax policy analysis (Table 3.4). Spain noted that Ministerial Departments send a report to the Secretary of State for Budgets and Expenditures analysing the gender impact of their spending programs. These reports form the basis for the formulation by the Secretary of State of the gender impact report (described in the section on implicit bias). Some countries that do not have specific gender budgeting requirements do consider the gender impact of all policies in other ways, including the impact of tax changes. For instance, Australia's government does not provide a statement specifically in relation to tax policy, but more broadly, in May 2021, as part of the 2021-22 budget, the government released a Women's Budget Statement (Government of Australia, 2021[34]). This statement includes analysis of the COVID-19 pandemic's impact on women, as well as an overview of key statistics relating to women's safety, economic security, and health and wellbeing. It details relevant budget initiatives, analysis, trends and existing government approaches. Luxembourg noted that every draft law and/or draft regulation must be accompanied by an impact assessment, in which one required category is gender neutrality.

Table 3.4. Does your country practise some form of gender budgeting?

Answer	Number	Share	Countries
Yes	19	44.2%	**Argentina**; **Austria**; Belgium; **Canada**; Finland; France; Germany; **Iceland**; Indonesia; Ireland; Italy; Kenya; Mexico; Montenegro; Peru; South Africa; Spain; **Sweden**; Ukraine
No	22	51.1%	Australia; Brazil; Costa Rica; Croatia; Estonia; Greece; Hungary; Israel; Latvia; Luxembourg; Netherlands, New Zealand; Norway; Portugal; Romania; San Marino; Saudi Arabia; Slovenia; Switzerland; Tunisia; United Kingdom; United States

Note: Countries in bold reported that their gender budgeting processes have specific requirements for tax policy.
Two countries (4.7%) did not reply to this question.
Source: OECD Tax & Gender Stocktaking Questionnaire 2021.

Figure 3.4. Use and legal basis or authority of gender budgeting of tax policy changes

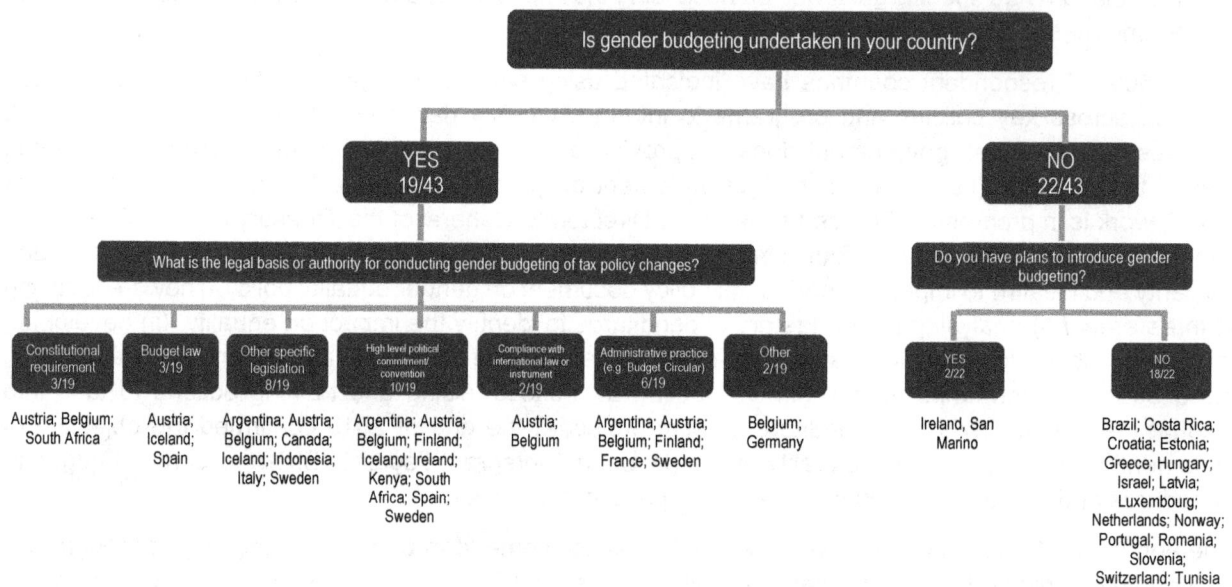

Source: OECD Tax & Gender Stocktaking Questionnaire 2021.

Among the countries that provided an answer regarding the legal basis for conducting gender budgeting of tax policy changes, Austria, Belgium and South Africa indicated that a constitutional requirement was the basis for this analysis. Austria indicated that men and women have equal rights under the Austrian Constitution. The state therefore promotes the actual implementation of equal rights for women and men and work towards the elimination of existing disadvantages. Belgium stated its introduction of a constitutional requirement in 2002. Despite some legal measures promoting gender equality since the 1980s, it was the first time the principle of equality between men and women had been explicitly affirmed (Article 10) (European Parliament, 2015[35]). In 1996, in South Africa, a commission of enquiry was established to ensure that the tax system supports the reduction of inequality and has no inherent bias against a specific group. Some countries do not consider that their constitution establishes a legal basis for conducting gender budgeting of tax policy changes but do consider that it helps to ensure gender equality. For instance, Kenya indicated that its Constitution recognises the rights of everyone and has entrenched Gender Equality as one of the key principle.

Eight other countries (Argentina,[6] Austria, Belgium, Canada, Iceland, Italy, Spain and Sweden) note that the basis for gender budgeting exists in their budget law or other legal frameworks. For example:

- Since 2013, the consideration of gender distortions in Austria has been embodied in the Budget Law, which ensures the implementation of the equality objectives in tax policy measures. Since that year, gender budgeting must be implemented at the federal level and the de facto equality between women and men must be considered in all stages of administrative action, from the formulation of objectives to their implementation and evaluation.

- Belgium reported having implemented in 2013 a 'gender test' (Government of Belgium, 2013[36]) a regulatory impact analysis which assesses the impact of regulatory proposals on women and men via a series of questions for policymakers.

- Canada enacted the Canada Gender Budgeting Act in 2018, enshrining the government's commitment to budget decision-making that takes into consideration the impacts of policies on all Canadians. These priorities range from addressing the gender wage gap to promoting more equal parenting roles and are associated with a set of goals and indicators to benchmark progress in achieving gender equality and diversity.

- In Germany, "gender mainstreaming" is included as a universal guiding principle in the Joint Rules of Procedure of the Federal Ministries, which state: 'Equality between men and women is a consistent guiding principle and should be promoted by all political, legislative and administrative actions of the Federal Ministries in their respective areas (gender mainstreaming)' (Government of Germany, 2020[37]).

- In Iceland, gender mainstreaming in policy making is required by the Act on Equal Status and Equal Rights Irrespective of Gender, also known as the "Gender Equality Act" (Government of Iceland, 2021[38]). The aim of this Act is to prevent discrimination on the basis of gender and to maintain equal status and equal opportunities for women and men, thus promoting gender equality in all spheres of society.

- A summary of Sweden's gender budgeting mainstreaming tool is set out in Box 3.2.

Box 3.2. Sweden's BUDGe for Gender Equality

BUDGe is a Swedish budgeting tool, in place since the early 2000s, that brings gender equality into the budget development process. It is an analytical tool which aims to help officials to determine whether a gender perspective is relevant for budget proposals, to conduct a gender analysis where so, and to account for the proposal's impact on gender equality.

The tool was developed within a broader government framework providing methods and models for gender mainstreaming. It was developed for the core activities of the Government Offices but has since been adapted to suit public agencies, municipalities and other organisations. It has five steps, as shown in the schematic below.

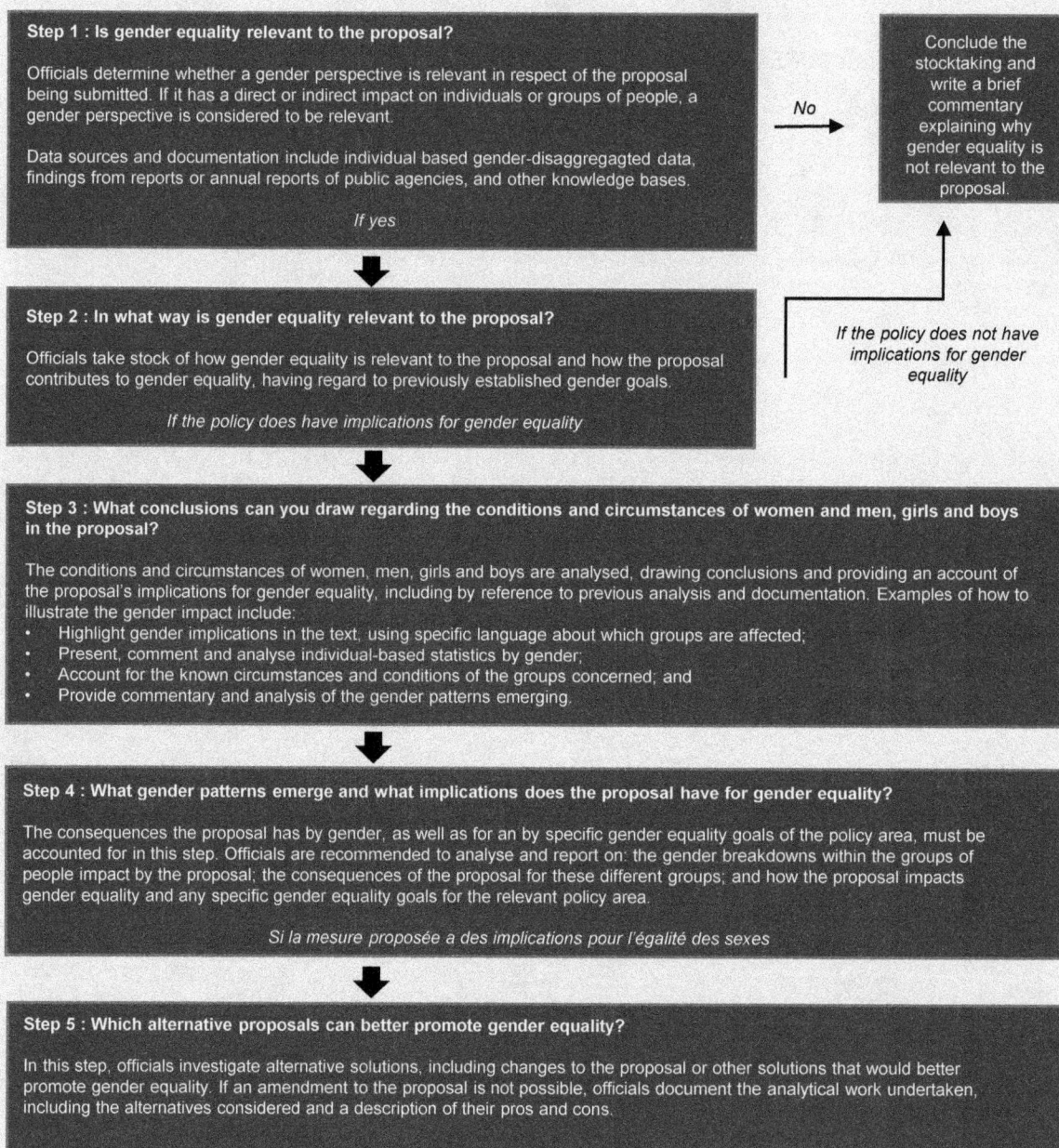

Step 1 : Is gender equality relevant to the proposal?

Officials determine whether a gender perspective is relevant in respect of the proposal being submitted. If it has a direct or indirect impact on individuals or groups of people, a gender perspective is considered to be relevant.

Data sources and documentation include individual based gender-disaggregated data, findings from reports or annual reports of public agencies, and other knowledge bases.

If yes

No → Conclude the stocktaking and write a brief commentary explaining why gender equality is not relevant to the proposal.

Step 2 : In what way is gender equality relevant to the proposal?

Officials take stock of how gender equality is relevant to the proposal and how the proposal contributes to gender equality, having regard to previously established gender goals.

If the policy does have implications for gender equality

If the policy does not have implications for gender equality

Step 3 : What conclusions can you draw regarding the conditions and circumstances of women and men, girls and boys in the proposal?

The conditions and circumstances of women, men, girls and boys are analysed, drawing conclusions and providing an account of the proposal's implications for gender equality, including by reference to previous analysis and documentation. Examples of how to illustrate the gender impact include:
- Highlight gender implications in the text, using specific language about which groups are affected;
- Present, comment and analyse individual-based statistics by gender;
- Account for the known circumstances and conditions of the groups concerned; and
- Provide commentary and analysis of the gender patterns emerging.

Step 4 : What gender patterns emerge and what implications does the proposal have for gender equality?

The consequences the proposal has by gender, as well as for an by specific gender equality goals of the policy area, must be accounted for in this step. Officials are recommended to analyse and report on: the gender breakdowns within the groups of people impact by the proposal; the consequences of the proposal for these different groups; and how the proposal impacts gender equality and any specific gender equality goals for the relevant policy area.

Si la mesure proposée a des implications pour l'égalité des sexes

Step 5 : Which alternative proposals can better promote gender equality?

In this step, officials investigate alternative solutions, including changes to the proposal or other solutions that would better promote gender equality. If an amendment to the proposal is not possible, officials document the analytical work undertaken, including the alternatives considered and a description of their pros and cons.

Source: https://government.se/information-material/2021/12/budge-for-gender--equality/ .

Austria and Belgium also indicated that compliance with international law or instruments constitute a legal basis or authority for conducting gender budgeting of tax policy changes.

The following figure shows the specific tools integrated by the 19 countries that include a gender budgeting process.

Figure 3.5. Specific tools or methods in which gender budgeting in relation to tax policy proposals

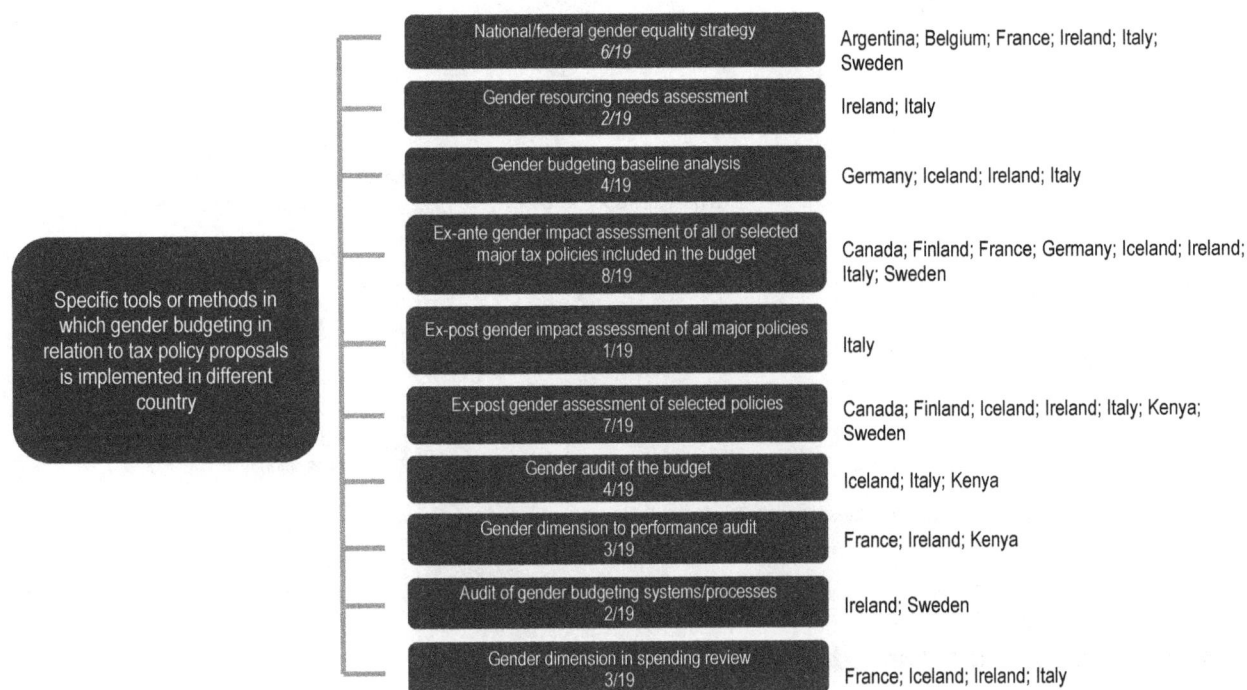

Specific tools or methods in which gender budgeting in relation to tax policy proposals is implemented in different country		
National/federal gender equality strategy 6/19	Argentina; Belgium; France; Ireland; Italy; Sweden
Gender resourcing needs assessment 2/19	Ireland; Italy
Gender budgeting baseline analysis 4/19	Germany; Iceland; Ireland; Italy
Ex-ante gender impact assessment of all or selected major tax policies included in the budget 8/19	Canada; Finland; France; Germany; Iceland; Ireland; Italy; Sweden
Ex-post gender impact assessment of all major policies 1/19	Italy
Ex-post gender assessment of selected policies 7/19	Canada; Finland; Iceland; Ireland; Italy; Kenya; Sweden
Gender audit of the budget 4/19	Iceland; Italy; Kenya
Gender dimension to performance audit 3/19	France; Ireland; Kenya
Audit of gender budgeting systems/processes 2/19	Ireland; Sweden
Gender dimension in spending review 3/19	France; Iceland; Ireland; Italy

Source: OECD Tax & Gender Stocktaking Questionnaire 2021.

Planned implementation of gender budgeting in relation to tax proposals

Two of the 22 countries that do not currently undertake gender budgeting indicated that official plans to introduce gender budgeting for tax policy proposals in the future are under consideration (Ireland and San Marino). In Ireland, in line with the OECD recommendations on an Equality Budget (OECD, 2019[39]), the country is considering how best to implement a parallel equality budgeting progress in respect to taxation, and set out an equality budgeting agenda of its current government programme (Government of Ireland, 2021[40]). In San Marino, the gender impact of tax measures is assessed when the legislative text is first forwarded to the San Marino body on Equal Opportunities, a delegation generally assigned to the Ministry of Health. San Marino are actively considering the introduction of gender budgeting in the near future.

In the United States, the current Administration established a working group across government agencies to advance the goal of expanding and refining Federal government data sets, including tax return data, for the purpose of measuring and promoting equity, including gender equity.

Figure 3.6. Summary of policy development process and gender budgeting

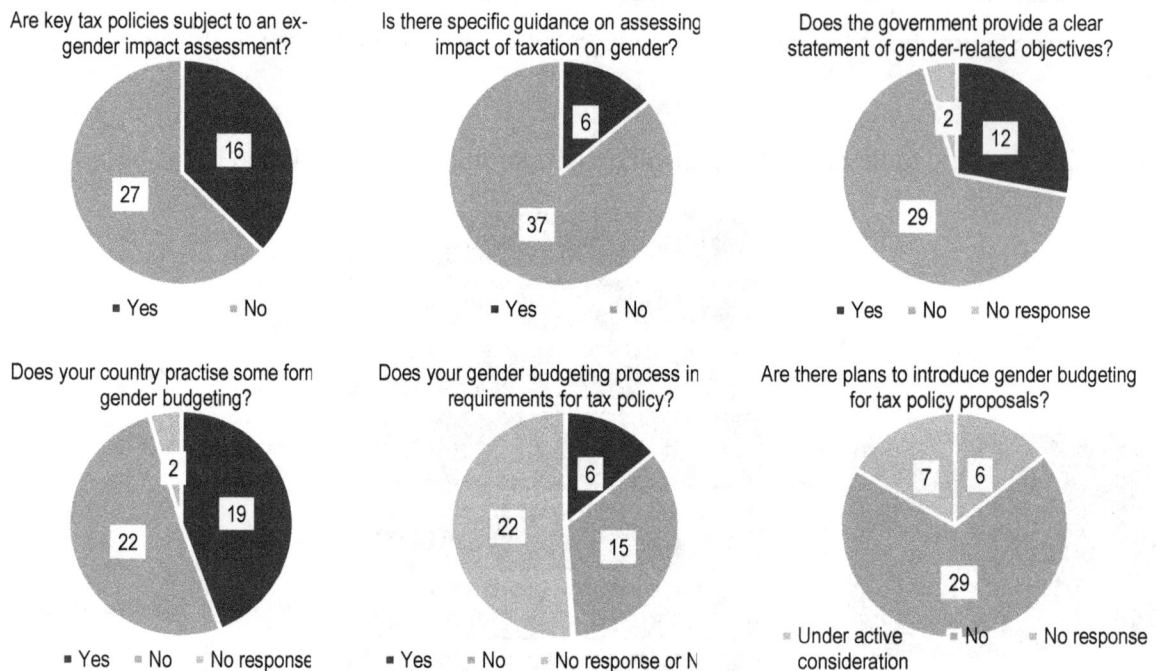

Are key tax policies subject to an ex-
gender impact assessment?

16

27

■ Yes　■ No

Is there specific guidance on assessing
impact of taxation on gender?

6

37

■ Yes　■ No

Does the government provide a clear
statement of gender-related objectives?

2

12

29

■ Yes　■ No　■ No response

Does your country practise some form
gender budgeting?

2

19

22

■ Yes　■ No　■ No response

Does your gender budgeting process in
requirements for tax policy?

6

22

15

■ Yes　■ No　■ No response or N

Are there plans to introduce gender budgeting
for tax policy proposals?

7　6

29

■ Under active　■ No　■ No response
consideration

Source: OECD Tax & Gender Stocktaking Questionnaire 2021.

StatLink ▆▆▆▆▆ https://stat.link/lu8qit

3.5. Tax compliance and administration

Tax compliance and administration can be analysed through a gender perspective. Understanding the compliance patterns of men and women through data collection, or undertaking a reflection on the gender implications of tax administration processes with a view to adapting some of them; can be useful to improve the tax system in light of the objective of gender equality and to address some of the biases observed. This section describes the country practices in relation to tax compliance and administration and makes a link with other existing studies and initiatives.

3.5.1. Overview of country practices in tax compliance and administration

Analysis of gender implications of tax administration or compliance

The vast majority of the countries surveyed (34 out of 43, i.e. 79%) indicated that they did not undertake any analysis on the gender implications of tax administration or compliance.

Table 3.5. Has your country undertaken any analysis on the gender implications of tax administration and compliance?

Answer	Number	Share	Countries
Yes	3	6.9%	Indonesia; New Zealand; Sweden
No	34	79.1%	Argentina; Belgium; Brazil; Canada; Costa Rica; Croatia; Finland; France; Germany; Greece; Hungary; Iceland; Ireland; Israel; Italy; Kenya; Latvia; Luxembourg; Mexico; Netherlands; Norway; Peru; Portugal; Romania; San Marino; Saudi Arabia; Slovenia; South Africa; Spain; Switzerland; Tunisia; United Kingdom; United States; Uruguay

Note: Six countries (13.9%) did not reply to this question.
Source: OECD Tax & Gender Stocktaking Questionnaire 2021.

Only three countries (7% of all respondents) indicated that they do undertake analysis on the gender implications of tax administration or compliance – Indonesia, New Zealand and Sweden:

- In 2006, Sweden's tax agency investigated the relationship between taxation and gender equality policy objectives, publishing a report in 2007 (Swedish Tax Agency, 2007[41]). The report describes policy measures that have an impact on gender equality, including joint taxation (Sweden adopted individual-based taxation, which was considered to have an income equalising effect), tax relief for domestic services (80% of these deductions were claimed by men), gross payroll deduction in exchange for tax-free benefit (more profitable to high earners, that are typically men). On compliance, it shows that since men are more likely to engage in business activities, they make more deductions from their earned income and declare higher capital gains than women, and thus make more errors in their declarations, and are therefore likely to be subject to tax audits, adjustments and penalties. The report concludes that the most effective measures are to simplify tax rules and to require gender-based analysis of these rules.

- A report from New Zealand's University of Wellington (González Cabral, Gemmell and Alinaghi, 2019[42]) examined patterns of non-compliance and under-reporting of income earned by self-employed individuals, indicating that there are gender differences in levels of non-compliance, and suggesting that males underreport more than females, which was observed consistently across income and expenditure variables.

Collection of gender-disaggregated data on tax compliance

The majority of countries surveyed do not collect gender-disaggregated data on tax compliance (22 out of 43, i.e. 51%). Eight countries (19%) indicated that they are "not aware" of whether such data are collected or not. Only seven countries (16%) responded that they do collect gender-disaggregated data: Argentina, Canada, France, Mexico, San Marino, Sweden and the United States.

Figure 3.7. Does your country collect gender-disaggregated data on tax compliance?

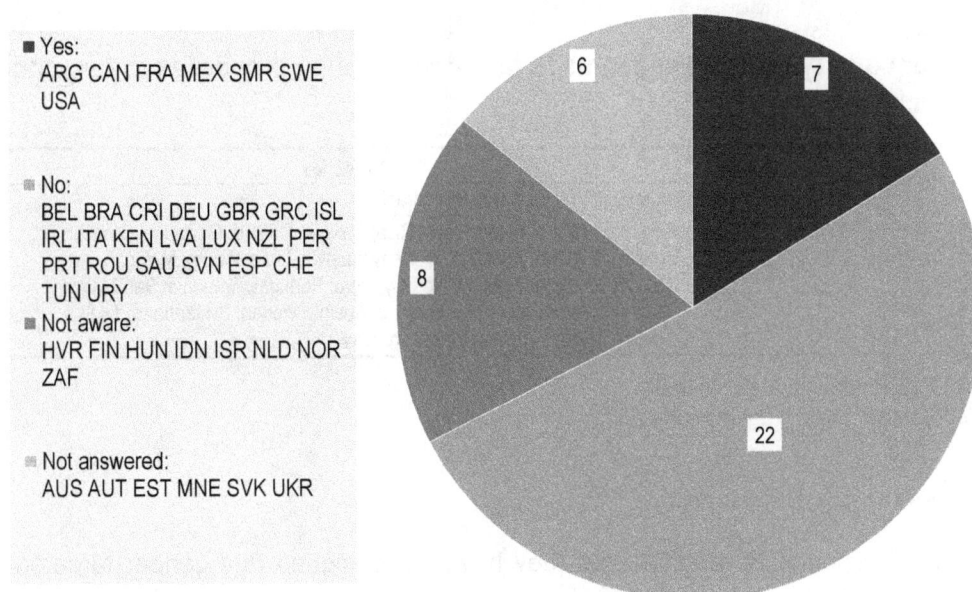

Yes:
ARG CAN FRA MEX SMR SWE USA

No:
BEL BRA CRI DEU GBR GRC ISL IRL ITA KEN LVA LUX NZL PER PRT ROU SAU SVN ESP CHE TUN URY

Not aware:
HVR FIN HUN IDN ISR NLD NOR ZAF

Not answered:
AUS AUT EST MNE SVK UKR

Source: OECD Tax & Gender Stocktaking Questionnaire 2021.

StatLink 🔗 https://stat.link/zif17o

- In 2020, Sweden published a report on tax reporting error (Swedish Tax Agency, 2021[43]), supplementing a report on the size and evolution of the tax gap and that contains gender-specific data on reporting error by types of taxes, based on the Swedish Tax Agency's statistical database of tax return data. The report shows, for instance, that between 2018 and 2020, the tax error resulting from incorrect deductions applied to employment income in tax returns is estimated at SEK 2.9 billion, of which women account for SEK 1.0 billion and men for SEK 1.9 billion.

- Canada also collects data on the number of returns by filing deadline and by gender, as well as on late-filing penalties assessed by gender. The data on late-filing show that the total and average penalties paid by men in 2017 are significantly higher than for women, whereas there are in total more tax returns submitted by women than men overall.

- In Mexico, gender-disaggregated data is used to analyse the impact of the tax structure on each gender.

- In the United States, data on gender and tax compliance are available but gender-specific compliance has not been assessed, although it may be included as a control variable in regression analyses.

Adjustments to tax administration processes in response to a specific gender's needs

The vast majority of countries surveyed reported that they have not made any adjustments to tax administration processes to respond to the needs of a specific gender (33 out of 43, i.e. 77%). Only four countries (9%) indicated that they have done so – Argentina, France, Indonesia and Israel. In Argentina, the Federal Administration of Public Revenues (AFIP) launched the Protocol for the Improvement of Comprehensive Attention to Citizens with an inclusive, federal and gender-based approach. This initiative promotes several channels to guarantee the inclusion of vulnerable sectors of the population. This new tool incorporates a gender perspective and cultural diversity. France stated that following the 2019 introduction of a withholding tax for personal income tax purposes, it is possible for a married or civil-union couple to opt for individualised rates rather than the household rate – noting that this option may be appropriate when there is a significant difference in income within the couple.

Table 3.6. Has your country made adjustments to tax administration processes to respond to the needs of a specific gender?

Answer	Number	Share	Countries
Yes	4	9.3%	Argentina; France; Indonesia; Israel
No	33	76.7%	Belgium; Brazil; Canada; Costa Rica; Croatia; Finland; Germany; Greece; Hungary; Iceland; Ireland; Italy; Kenya; Latvia; Luxembourg; Mexico; Netherlands; New Zealand; Norway; Peru; Portugal; Romania; San Marino; Saudi Arabia; Slovenia; South Africa; Spain; Sweden; Switzerland; Tunisia; United Kingdom; United States; Uruguay

Note: Six countries (13.9%) did not reply to this question
Source: OECD Tax & Gender Stocktaking Questionnaire 2021.

Gender-targeted taxpayer awareness campaigns

The vast majority of respondents reported that they have not designed any gender targeted taxpayer education or awareness campaigns (32 out of 43, i.e. 74%). In many of these countries, this may be due to the fact that awareness campaigns are typically directed at individual taxpayers more generally, although not specifically targeted at one gender, for example in Tunisia.

Five countries (12%) indicated that they have done so, although in most cases these campaigns are gender-neutral in their own right but the underlying service or programme is primarily used by one gender

(Argentina, Canada, Indonesia, New Zealand and the United States). For example, Canada has put in place a programme to help modest-income individuals file their tax returns and access tax benefits (the "Community Volunteer Income Tax Program"), which, even if not targeted at women in particular, has been used by women in difficult situations. New Zealand also implemented an awareness campaign for a tax credit ("Best Start") directed at families that have a new-born baby (Government of New Zealand, 2021[44]).

Figure 3.8. Has your country-designed gender targeted taxpayer education/awareness campaigns?

Number of countries

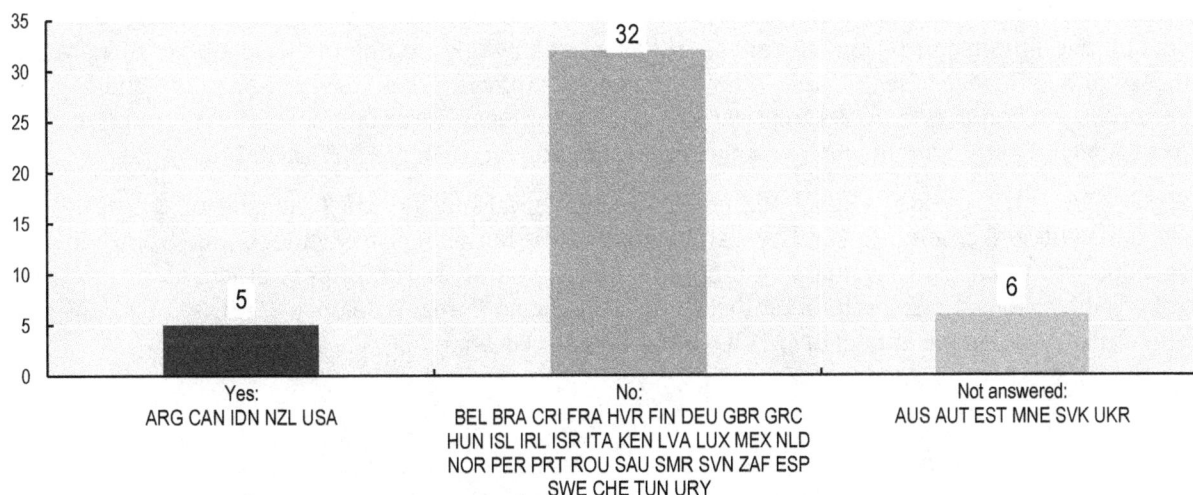

Source: OECD Tax & Gender Stocktaking Questionnaire 2021.

StatLink ﮔﺱ https://stat.link/bnofat

3.5.2. General observations on gender equity in tax compliance and administration

A clear trend is observed among the countries responding to the survey: the overwhelming majority indicated that they have not undertaken analyses on the gender impact of tax administration and compliance measures, and that they have not adjusted their tax administration processes in response to the needs of a specific gender, nor have they launched taxpayer awareness campaigns directed at a particular gender. However, the small number of countries that have implemented such initiatives and reported on them through the questionnaire have provided interesting data on their findings and analyses.

The answers provided by countries could reflect the lack of gender disaggregated data on tax compliance and administration, which appears to be confirmed by a vast majority of respondents – with 70% of the respondents indicating that they do not collect such data or are not aware if they do, which means in any case that they do not currently have access to it. As for other aspects of the tax and gender work, the lack of such data may be an obstacle to a deeper analysis. The answers could also mean that the analysis of tax compliance and administration by gender type has not yet emerged as an area of priority for many countries.

Going forward, further analysis of tax administration and compliance measures and their impact on gender could draw on additional and external sources to complement the information provided by countries. The activities and outcomes of the OECD Forum on Tax Administration's Gender Balance Network may be useful in this regard (see Box 3). Several studies and reports suggest that women have higher levels of tax compliance than men globally (OECD, 2019[45]) (D'Attoma, Malézieux, Volintiru, 2020[46]) (Kangave, Sebaggala, Waiswa, 2021[47]),

---

Box 3.3. The OECD Forum on Tax Administration's Gender Balance Network

The OECD's Forum on Tax Administration (FTA) brings together Commissioners from over 53 advanced and emerging tax administrations. It has a broad work programme which looks to increase fairness and effectiveness of tax administration. Commissioners recognised that there was underrepresentation of women in senior executive roles in many FTA countries and female staff remain proportionally underrepresented in executive positions (see Fig. 9.9. of (OECD, 2021[48])).

In 2019, FTA Commissioners launched the Gender Balance Network, which aims to be a catalyst for positive institutional change to improve gender balance in tax administration leadership positions by developing mentoring and secondment programmes as well as exploring best practices across FTA member jurisdictions including through the study Advancing Gender Balance (OECD, 2020[49]), and through reflections on the impact of COVID-19 on Gender Balance (OECD, 2020[50]).

Source: OECD Forum on Tax Administration.

3.6. Data on gender and taxation available for use in analysis

Gender differentiated data and information is critical for policymaking as it facilitates the assessment and development of appropriate evidence-based responses and corrective actions. For governments to include the impact of taxes on gender as key dimensions in their tax policy, access to quality gender-disaggregated micro-data is needed.

This section outlays the survey findings on the availability and quality of gender-differentiated data. The survey shows a mixed picture in terms of data availability. While most countries do have at least some disaggregated data available, availability of detailed micro-data on wealth, assets and property ownership and, micro-data on male and female consumption appears to be a particular challenge for many countries.

Twenty-five of the 43 countries, representing 58% of the respondents, had disaggregated data available for policy analysis. This data was available across various taxes, such as PIT, SSCs, VAT/GST, capital or property taxes. In Spain, gender-disaggregated data and statistics are available to the tax authority in relation to PIT (Ministerio de Hacienda, n.d.[51]), wealth taxes (Ministerio de Hacienda, n.d.[52]) (Agencia Tributaria, 2018[53]) and SSCs. In some countries, such as Croatia, gender disaggregated data is available in the main registry of taxpayers of the tax administration. In Ireland, gender is a recorded field on revenue administration systems and is used as a basis to report on tax returns for different genders (Acheson and Collins, 2020[54]). In Australia, gender disaggregated data is retrievable from the individual's income, including private pension information. In numerous instances, data on gender could not be accessed from Corporate Income Taxes (CIT) and VAT/GST owing to the challenge of linking the large entities to individual owners. For few countries, for instance in Luxembourg, gender disaggregated data is not directly available. Some countries reported inferencing such data from the titles such as (Mr., Ms.). However, this form of referencing poses a limitation, as such titles do not directly map to a specific gender.

Table 3.7. Is gender-disaggregated data available from tax returns for use in policy analysis?

Answer	Number	Share	Countries
Yes	25	58.1%	Argentina; Australia; Austria; Belgium; Brazil; Canada; Finland; France; Greece; Hungary ; Iceland; Israel; Italy; Luxembourg; Mexico; Netherlands; Norway; San Marino; Slovenia; South Africa; Spain; Sweden; United Kingdom; United States; Uruguay
No	12	27.9%	Costa Rica; Germany; Indonesia; Ireland; Kenya; Latvia; Peru; Portugal ; Romania; Saudi Arabia; Switzerland; Tunisia
Other	2	4.7%	Croatia; New Zealand

Note: In the United States, although gender information is not directly collected by tax returns, taxpayer identification numbers can be linked to other administrative data to draw conclusions on gender and income levels. Four countries (9.3%) did not reply to this question.
Source: OECD Tax & Gender Stocktaking Questionnaire 2021.

The level of data disaggregation for 16 countries is at the individual level or individual micro-data. This is attributed to the fact that every form of data (from PIT, SSCs, tax registries) can be linked to the individual taxpayer allowing for the analysis of the tax framework across a range of dimensions, such as age, economic sectors, gender and income level.

For 14 of the 25 countries that have gender-disaggregated data, uptake of tax incentives and benefits can be measured on a gender basis in the areas of taxation where the data was available.

3.6.1. Access to gender-disaggregated non-tax data for policy analysis[7]

From the results obtained, countries had varying access to different forms of gender-disaggregated non-tax data. However, countries' data availability clustered in some forms of data. For instance, information on male and female income was markedly more accessible than that on consumption or property and wealth ownership. While in no area was there uniform access to disaggregated data, these findings highlight the areas where differentiated data appears to be especially challenging to access, which are discussed further below. The main sources of the non-tax data were indicated to be the tax registries and specific government surveys.

Detailed micro-data on male and female incomes is available to 24 of the 43 respondent countries (56%), both separately and within households. Countries indicated a number of sources from which this detailed information is derived:

- In Sweden, this data is accessible from tax data;
- In Australia, household surveys such as the Australian Bureau of Statistics (ABS) Survey of Income and Housing (SIH), ABS Census of population of Housing and the Household, Income and Labour Dynamics in Australia (HILDA) survey provide detailed information on household income;
- In Luxembourg, even though this data is accessible, it is not directly available and, as such, is derived from inferencing;
- In the United States, detailed microdata on male and female incomes, as well as participation in businesses, is available from the Current Population Survey.
- In Spain, the data is available from the Survey on Living Conditions (Instituto Nacional de Estadística, 2020[55]).

Figure 3.9. Do you have access to the following gender disaggregated non-tax data available for policy analysis?

Number of countries reporting detailed microdata on male and female

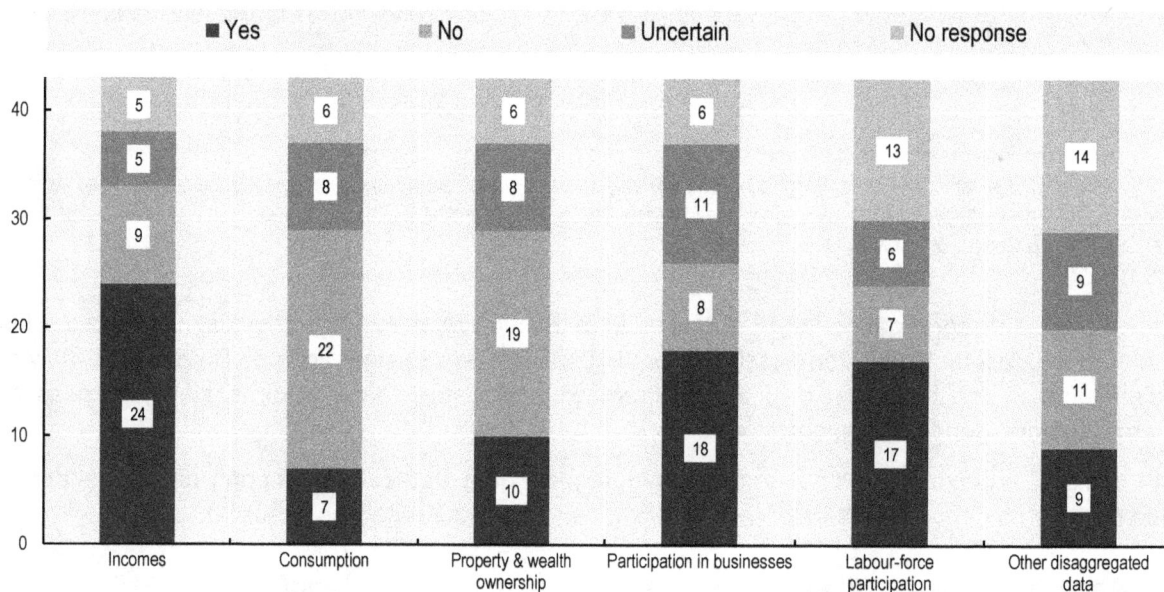

Legend: ■ Yes | ■ No | ■ Uncertain | ■ No response

Category	Yes	No	Uncertain	No response
Incomes	24	9	5	5
Consumption	7	22	8	6
Property & wealth ownership	10	19	8	6
Participation in businesses	18	8	11	6
Labour-force participation	17	7	6	13
Other disaggregated data	9	11	9	14

Source: OECD Tax & Gender Stocktaking Questionnaire 2021.

StatLink ▨▧⤷ https://stat.link/dkpf2e

In contrast, only six countries have access to detailed micro-data on male and female consumption. Most of the available data is from surveys, which collect information on household expenditure providing consumption by household but not on an individual level/individual microdata.

Only ten of the 43 countries have access to detailed microdata on male and female property and wealth ownership. It seems that such data is unavailable at microdata level but is present on household level.

Eighteen of the 43 countries have access to information on men's and women's participation in business. This data is available from a range of sources, including tax registries, labour force surveys and household surveys. In Australia, information from the ABS Labour Force Survey provides a detailed breakdown of labour force participation, which is available by industry sector and allows the identification of self-employed individuals. Additionally, household surveys allow identification of income from unincorporated businesses providing data on individual's participation in business. Spain also has access to data on women's employment and presence on companies' boards of directors.

Seventeen of the 43 countries have access to information on male and female labour-force participation (hours worked, wages, unemployment, sectoral involvement) representing 40% of the total respondents. For instance, Spain noted that it has access to data related to the labour market as well as on education and culture, health, security and justice, social analysis and electoral processes.

3.7. Usability of gender-disaggregated data in practice

Even where data is available, there are concerns about its usability (Table 3.8). Only nine countries confirmed the data was fit for purpose, a further 16 indicated the data was useable with caveats or extrapolations, while five countries indicated while data was available; it was not fit for purpose.

Australia stated that the data listed is available for use within the Treasury for policy development and that much of this data is available to approved researchers in unit record data, or summarised in freely available publications.

Table 3.8. How usable is the available gender-disaggregated data in practice?

Answer	Number	Share	Countries
Able to be used with caveats	11	25.6%	Austria; Finland; France; Hungary; Ireland; Italy; Netherlands; New Zealand; Saudi Arabia; Sweden; United Kingdom
Able to be used with caveats, extrapolations	1	2.3%	Belgium
Extrapolations	5	11.6%	Croatia; Indonesia; Peru; Romania; San Marino
Fit for purpose	9	20.9%	Canada; Iceland; Israel; Kenya; Mexico; Norway; South Africa, Spain; United States
Not fit for purpose	5	11.6%	Brazil; Germany; Greece, Luxembourg; Slovenia

Note: Twelve countries (28%) did not reply to this question.
Source: OECD Tax & Gender Stocktaking Questionnaire 2021.

Countries surveyed prioritised the need for certain forms of gender-disaggregated data in their responses. There was a recurring emphasis on the need for access to microdata on wealth, assets and property ownership by gender. This was mentioned by Belgium, Iceland, Mexico, South Africa, Sweden and the United Kingdom, echoing the findings of the significant gap on gender-disaggregated data on wealth and ownership. Additionally, Iceland, Kenya, Saudi Arabia, South Africa, and Uruguay highlighted the need for microdata/individual level data on consumption patterns.

Different countries indicated different measures to improve access to gender-related data in line with their needs. Germany stated the need for explicit questions in PIT returns, which would allow unambiguous assignment of income. Mexico mentioned that improved systematisation of the production or generation of tax databases disaggregated by gender for decision-making would improve the gender-disaggregated data quality. This was reiterated by Peru and San Marino who indicated the need for access to information and improved IT systems, respectively. The United Kingdom highlighted the need for disaggregating by protected characteristics and gender, which reinforces the need for data on income, wealth, employment and labour market participation disaggregated at gender and ethnicity levels. Saudi Arabia indicated that access to gender disaggregated data could be improved by requiring banks to collect and provide such information. Spain noted that including a gender variable in all the surveys carried out at the National Statistical Institute and the various ministries could result in more complete data in the medium term.

3.8. Country priorities and next steps

Finally, the survey asked countries to indicate their three main priorities for future work on tax policy and gender issues out of a range of options.

The top priority (identified by ten respondent jurisdictions) was consideration of the impact of tax credit or tax allowance provisions on gender equity. Among these countries, Belgium indicated the importance of considering the impact of tax credits and allowances on the distribution of unpaid work (e.g. childcare, parental care, household chores), and Israel emphasised the impact of gender bias both in and out of the tax system, in particular via tax credits and allowances, as well as SSCs, which provide incentives for women to undertake unpaid childcare and reduce working hours. The second most common priority was consideration of explicit bias to promote gender equity (nine countries).

Out of the top five options chosen by countries, three related to further analysis on the impact of labour taxation. Alongside the impact of tax credits and allowances on gender (ten countries), the progressivity of the PIT system was seen to be a priority by eight countries. The tax treatment of second earners was indicated as a priority by six countries. A further five countries highlighted the impact of SSCs on gender outcomes as a priority for further work. Of these countries, South Africa noted the potential for SSCs (e.g. earned income tax credits) as a possible means to ameliorate the gendered impacts of labour force participation; and the United Kingdom highlighted that the lower incomes of women, as well as maternity leave provisions, may lead women to accrue lower SSCs than men. Further work on the impact of labour taxes and SSCs on gender could build on prior OECD work, including (Thomas and O'Reilly, 2016[56]), and (OECD, 2016[57]).

After the taxation of labour income, exploring gender bias in wealth and inheritance (six countries), the taxation of capital income (five countries) and SMEs (five countries), as well as the impact of VAT/GST on gender equity (five countries) were seen as the next priorities. While tax compliance was seen as a priority area by five countries, tax administration (two countries) was a comparatively lower priority. No countries indicated that excises or trade taxes were a priority for future work.

In addition to the priorities included in the survey, Canada suggested that future work could be at a higher level, by providing countries with a suggested framework for analysis, reporting and gender equality goal setting. This would have the goal of providing countries with guidelines and best practices for detailed reporting and could also facilitate easier data collection and compilations by the OECD and other organizations interested in cross-country comparisons.

Finally, one country indicated that future work on gender was not a priority.

Figure 3.10. Country priorities for future work

Number of countries responding (more than one response was possible per country)

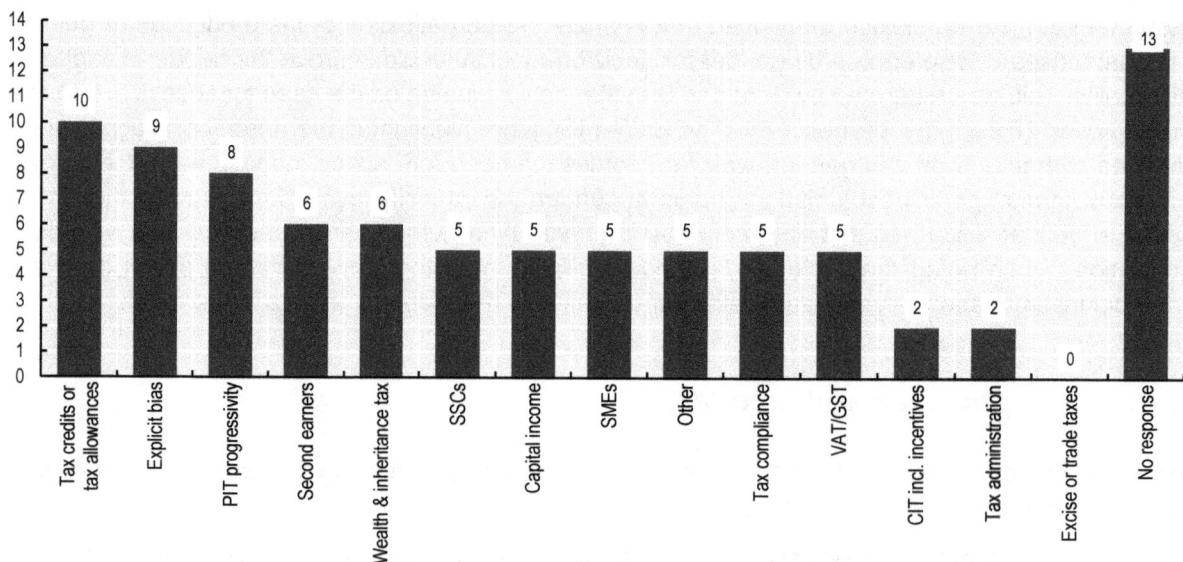

Source: OECD Tax & Gender Stocktaking Questionnaire 2021.

StatLink 🔗 https://stat.link/js1oe2

References

Acheson and Collins (2020), *Gender and Pay in Revenue*, [54]
    https://www.revenue.ie/en/corporate/documents/research/gender-pay-2020.pdf (accessed on
    22 October 2021).

Agencia Tributaria (2018), *Resumen del Impuesto port Comunidades Autónomas*, [53]
    https://www.agenciatributaria.es/AEAT/Contenidos_Comunes/La_Agencia_Tributaria/Estadist
    icas/Publicaciones/sites/patrimonio/2018/jrubikf70a09195f09fc7e9169b1a102d15880e53afb3
    e4.html (accessed on 13 January 2022).

BBVA (2020), *La pandemia ha ampliado la brecha de género en el mercado laboral español*, [16]
    https://www.bbva.com/es/el-impacto-de-la-pandemia-en-el-mercado-laboral-ha-ampliado-la-
    brecha-de-genero-en-espana-segun-bbva-research/ (accessed on 13 January 2022).

Castellanos-Torres, E., J. Mateos and E. Chilet-Rosell (2020), "COVID-19 en clave de género", [17]
    Gaceta Sanitaria, Vol. 34/5, pp. 419-421, http://dx.doi.org/10.1016/J.GACETA.2020.04.007.

Center on Budget and Policy Priorities (2019), *Policy Basics: The Earned Income Tax Credit |* [29]
    Center on Budget and Policy Priorities, https://www.cbpp.org/research/federal-tax/the-earned-
    income-tax-credit (accessed on 11 January 2022).

Congress of Argentina (2020), *Regime for the Promotion of the Knowledge Economy (Law* [18]
    27570), https://www.argentina.gob.ar/normativa/nacional/ley-27570-343520/texto (accessed
    on 16 January 2022).

D'Attoma, Malézieux, Volintiru (2020), "Gender, Social Value Orientation, and Tax Compliance", [46]
    http://dx.doi.org/10.1093/cesifo/ifz016.

Debitoor (2021), *Ayudas para mujeres autónomas*, https://debitoor.es/guia-pequenas- [23]
    empresas/autonomos/ayudas-para-mujeres-autonomas (accessed on 13 January 2022).

Department of the Treasury, U.S. (2015), *The Income Tax Treatment of Married Couples*, [27]
    https://home.treasury.gov/system/files/131/Two-Earner-Penalty-and-Marginal-Tax-Rates.pdf
    (accessed on 11 January 2022).

Doorley (2018), *Taxation, Work and Gender Equality in Ireland*, https://ftp.iza.org/dp11495.pdf [12]
    (accessed on 21 October 2021).

Doorley, O'Donoghue and Sologon (2021), *The Gender Gap in Income and the COVID-19* [21]
    Pandemic, https://www.iza.org/en/publications/dp/14360/the-gender-gap-in-income-and-the-
    covid-19-pandemic (accessed on 21 October 2021).

European Parliament (2015), *The policy on gender equality in Belgium*, [35]
    http://publications.europa.eu/resource/cellar/f277eaae-977c-4929-8ab8-
    a5fdf368b073.0001.01/DOC_1 (accessed on 22 October 2021).

Federal Public Service Finance of Belgium (2021), *Coparentalité | SPF Finances*, [11]
    https://finances.belgium.be/fr/particuliers/famille/situation_familiale/coparentalite (accessed
    on 21 October 2021).

French National Assembly (2014), *N° 1875 - Rapport d'information de Mme Catherine Coutelle déposé par la délégation de l'Assemblée nationale aux droits des femmes et à l'égalité des chances entre les hommes et les femmes sur la question des femmes et du système fiscal*, https://www.assemblee-nationale.fr/14/rap-info/i1875.asp (accessed on 3 December 2021). [31]

González Cabral, Gemmell and Alinaghi (2019), "Are Survey-Based Self-Employment Income Under-Reporting Estimates Biased? New Evidence from Matched Register and Survey Data", https://www.wgtn.ac.nz/sacl/centres-and-chairs/cpf/publications/working-papers (accessed on 22 October 2021). [42]

Government of Australia (2021), *Women's Budget Statement 2021-22*, https://budget.gov.au/2021-22/content/womens-statement/download/womens_budget_statement_2021-22.pdf (accessed on 22 October 2021). [34]

Government of Belgium (2013), *Analyse d'impact intégrée*, https://igvm-iefh.belgium.be/sites/default/files/downloads/Formulaire%20AIR.doc. [36]

Government of Canada (2020), *GBA+ Summary for Canada's COVID-19 Economic Response Plan*, https://www.canada.ca/en/department-finance/services/publications/economic-fiscal-snapshot/gba-summary-economic-response-plan.html (accessed on 21 October 2021). [22]

Government of Germany (2020), *Joint Rules of Procedure of the Federal Ministries (GGO)*, https://www.bmi.bund.de/SharedDocs/downloads/EN/themen/moderne-verwaltung/ggo_en.pdf?__blob=publicationFile&v=6 (accessed on 27 October 2021). [37]

Government of Iceland (2021), *About Gender Equality*, https://www.government.is/topics/human-rights-and-equality/equality/about-gender-equality/ (accessed on 22 October 2021). [38]

Government of Ireland (2021), *Programme for Government: Our Shared Future*, https://www.gov.ie/en/publication/7e05d-programme-for-government-our-shared-future/ (accessed on 22 October 2021). [40]

Government of New Zealand (2021), *Working for Families payments*, https://www.govt.nz/browse/family-and-whanau/financial-help-for-your-family/working-for-families-payments/ (accessed on 22 October 2021). [44]

Government of Sweden (2020), *Fördelningspolitisk redogörelse*, https://www.regeringen.se/4a6b9b/contentassets/cec99f9b7f3a4ded95422348904e499c/fordelningspolitisk-redogorelse.pdf (accessed on 21 October 2021). [3]

Harding, M., D. Paturot and H. Simon (2022 (forthcoming)), *Taxation of Part-time Work*, OECD Taxation Working Paper. [5]

INSEE (2019), *Imposition des couples et des familles : effets budgétaires et redistributifs de l'impôt sur le revenu*, https://www.insee.fr/fr/statistiques/4253854 (accessed on 3 December 2021). [6]

Instituto de la Mujer (2007), "Informes de Impact de Género", https://www.inmujeres.gob.es/publicacioneselectronicas/documentacion/Documentos/DE0259.pdf (accessed on 13 January 2022). [30]

Instituto Nacional de Estadística (2020), *Life Conditions Survey*, https://www.ine.es/dyngs/INEbase/en/operacion.htm?c=Estadistica_C&cid=1254736176807&menu=ultiDatos&idp=1254735976608 (accessed on 13 January 2022). [55]

International Development Research Centre (2010), *Taxation and gender equity: a comparative analysis of direct and indirect taxes in developing and developed countries*. [33]

Italian Ministry of Economy and Finance (2019), *2019 Gender Budget Report -Summary and main results*, https://www.rgs.mef.gov.it/_Documenti/VERSIONE-I/Attivit--i/Rendiconto/Bilancio-di-genere/2019/Summary-and-main-results_BdG_-2019.pdf (accessed on 21 October 2021). [2]

Kangave, Sebaggala, Waiswa (2021), *Are Women More Tax Compliant than Men? How Would We Know?*, http://dx.doi.org/10.19088/ICTD.2021.006. [47]

Kidwingira, Mshana, Okyere (2011), "Taxation and gender: Why does it matter?", *Tax Justice Network Africa*, http://taxjusticeafrica.net/index.php?option=com_ (accessed on 21 October 2021). [1]

LaLumia, S. (2008), "The effects of joint taxation of married couples on labor supply and non-wage income", *Journal of Public Economics*, Vol. 92/7, pp. 1698-1719, https://ideas.repec.org/a/eee/pubeco/v92y2008i7p1698-1719.html (accessed on 11 January 2022). [7]

Lin, E. and P. Tong (2014), "Effects of Marriage Penalty Relief Tax Policy on Marriage Taxes and Marginal Tax Rates of Cohabiting Couples", *Proceedings. Annual Conference on Taxation and Minutes of the Annual Meeting of the National Tax Association*, Vol. 107, https://www.jstor.org/stable/26812158?seq=1#metadata_info_tab_contents (accessed on 11 January 2022). [28]

Ministerio de Economía (2021), *Perspectiva de Género en la modificación del Impuesto a las Ganancias Sociedades*, https://www.argentina.gob.ar/economia/politicatributaria/observatorio-de-tributacion-y-genero/perspectiva-de-genero-en-la (accessed on 16 January 2022). [19]

Ministerio de Economía (2021), *Presupuesto 2021. Primer presupuesto con Perspectiva de Género y Diversidad. La construcción de una herramienta para la igualdad*, https://www.argentina.gob.ar/sites/default/files/presupuesto_2021._primer_presupuesto_con_perspectiva_de_genero_y_diversidad.pdf (accessed on 31 January 2022). [58]

Ministerio de Economía (2021), *Registradas. Más empleo y más derechos para las trabajadoras de casas particulares*, https://www.argentina.gob.ar/sites/default/files/2021/11/registradas_-_mas_empleo_y_mas_derechos_para_tcp_ok.pdf (accessed on 31 January 2022). [14]

Ministerio de Economía (2021), *Seguimiento del gasto vinculado con políticas de género en el presupuesto nacional del Tercer Trimestre de 2021*, https://dgsiaf.mecon.gov.ar/wp-content/uploads/genero-trimestral-informe_2021_2.pdf (accessed on 31 January 2022). [20]

Ministerio de Hacienda (n.d.), *El Impuesto sobre el Patrimonio*, https://www.hacienda.gob.es/es-ES/Areas%20Tematicas/Impuestos/Direccion%20General%20de%20Tributos/Paginas/Estadisticas_IP.aspx (accessed on 13 January 2022). [52]

Ministerio de Hacienda (n.d.), *El Impuesto sobre la Renta de las Personas Físicas*, [51]
https://www.hacienda.gob.es/es-ES/Areas%20Tematicas/Impuestos/Direccion%20General%20de%20Tributos/Paginas/Estadisticas_IRPF.aspx (accessed on 13 January 2022).

Ministry of Health, K. (2019), *Menstrual Hygiene Management Policy*, [25]
https://www.health.go.ke/wp-content/uploads/2020/05/MHM-Policy-11-May-2020.pdf (accessed on 21 October 2021).

OECD (2021), *Tax Administration 2021: Comparative Information on OECD and other Advanced and Emerging Economies*, OECD Publishing, Paris, https://dx.doi.org/10.1787/cef472b9-en. [48]

OECD (2020), *Advancing Gender Balance in the Workforce: A Collective Responsibility*, [49]
https://www.oecd.org/tax/forum-on-tax-administration/publications-and-products/advancing-gender-balance-in-the-workforce-a-collective-responsibility.pdf (accessed on 3 November 2021).

OECD (2020), *Consumption Tax Trends 2020*, https://www.oecd-ilibrary.org/taxation/consumption-tax-trends-2020_152def2d-en (accessed on 21 October 2021). [24]

OECD (2020), "Gender Balance and COVID-19", https://www.oecd.org/tax/forum-on-tax-administration/publications-and-products/letter-gender-balance-network-covid19-risks-challenges-opportunities.pdf (accessed on 3 November 2021). [50]

OECD (2019), "Equality Budgeting in Ireland", https://www.oecd.org/gov/budgeting/equality-budgeting-in-ireland.pdf (accessed on 22 October 2021). [39]

OECD (2019), *OECD Economic Surveys - Japan*, OECD Publishing, Paris, https://www.oecd-ilibrary.org/docserver/fd63f374-en.pdf?expires=1642079950&id=id&accname=ocid84004878&checksum=F2BB9274A47F358BEEFBF2C48427A05F (accessed on 13 January 2022). [9]

OECD (2019), *Part-time and Partly Equal: Gender and Work in the Netherlands*, OECD Publishing, Paris, https://dx.doi.org/10.1787/204235cf-en. [4]

OECD (2019), *Tax Morale: What Drives People and Businesses to Pay Tax?*, OECD Publishing, Paris, https://dx.doi.org/10.1787/f3d8ea10-en. [45]

OECD (2016), *Taxing Wages 2016*, https://www.oecd-ilibrary.org/taxation/taxing-wages-2016_tax_wages-2016-en (accessed on 21 October 2021). [8]

OECD (2016), *Taxing Wages 2016*, OECD Publishing, Paris, https://dx.doi.org/10.1787/tax_wages-2016-en. [57]

Olken, S. (2011), "Informal Taxation", *American Economic Journal: Applied Economics*, pp. 1-28, http://dx.doi.org/10.1257/app.3.4.1. [13]

Orsini (2005), "The 2001 Belgian Tax Reform: Equity and Efficiency", http://www.econ.kuleuven.be/ces/discussionpapers/default.htm (accessed on 22 October 2021). [10]

Riihelä, V. (2015), *Veromuutosten vaikutukset sukupuolen mukaan vuosina 1993–2012*, https://www.doria.fi/bitstream/handle/10024/148718/t180.pdf?sequence=1&isAllowed=y (accessed on 22 October 2021). [32]

Stotsky, J. (1996), *Gender Bias in Tax Systems*, https://papers.ssrn.com/abstract=882995 (accessed on 13 May 2021). [26]

Swedish Tax Agency (2021), *Skattefelsrapport 2020 - Underlagsrapport till årsredovisningen avseende skattefelets storlek och utveckling*, https://www.ekobrottsmyndigheten.se/wp-content/uploads/2021/03/underlagsrapport-skattefelet-2020.pdf (accessed on 22 October 2021). [43]

Swedish Tax Agency (2007), *Enklare skatter för ökad jämställdhet? Beskattningen och de jämställdhetspolitiska målen*, https://docplayer.se/10629622-Enklare-skatter-for-okad-jamstalldhet-beskattningen-och-de-jamstalldhetspolitiska-malen-rapport-2007-2-skatteverket.html (accessed on 22 October 2021). [41]

Thomas, A. and P. O'Reilly (2016), *The Impact of Tax and Benefit Systems on the Workforce Participation Incentives of Women*, OECD Tax Working Paper, https://www.oecd-ilibrary.org/taxation/the-impact-of-tax-and-benefit-systems-on-the-workforce-participation-incentives-of-women_d950acfc-en (accessed on 13 May 2021). [56]

UNICEF and DNEIyG (2021), *Desafíos de las políticas públicas frente a la crisis de los cuidados. El impacto de la pandemia en los hogares con niños, niñas y adolescentes a cargo de mujeres*, https://www.argentina.gob.ar/sites/default/files/hogares_pandemia_final_29.04.pdf (accessed on 31 January 2022). [15]

Notes

1 Brazil, Canada, Costa Rica, Croatia, Germany, Greece, Hungary, Ireland, Israel, Italy, Kenya, Latvia, Luxembourg, Montenegro, New Zealand, Peru, Romania, San Marino, Saudi Arabia, the Slovak Republic, Slovenia, Tunisia and Ukraine.

2 Argentina, Australia, Austria, Belgium, Estonia, France, Iceland, Indonesia, Mexico, the Netherlands, South Africa, Spain, Sweden, Switzerland, the United Kingdom, Uruguay and the United States.

3 A similar figure was provided by Spain, noting that women represent the household member with the lowest income in 84% of the cases.

4 https://www.iberley.es/temas/tarifa-plana-nuevos-trabajadores-autonomos-alta-reta-2801.

5 Australia, Austria, Belgium, Canada, Finland, France, Iceland, Ireland, Italy, the Netherlands, Spain, Sweden, the United Kingdom, the United States and Uruguay.

6 (Ministerio de Economía, 2021[58]).

7 See Annex A for a detailed list of countries.

4 Conclusions and implications

The impact of taxation on gender outcomes is widely considered to be important across the countries surveyed. Three-quarters of the 43 countries who responded consider tax & gender to be at least somewhat important (Figure 3.1), with eight of these countries considering it to be very important. Twenty-two countries indicated that they have implemented specific tax reforms to improve gender equity. These measures have typically been implemented in the personal income tax system, either via changes to the unit of taxation or administration or the inclusion of credits or allowances, although several countries have also introduced zero or reduced VAT rates for sanitary products with the goal of improving the gender impacts of the tax system.

Few countries noted examples of explicit bias in their tax system, either now or on a historic basis, also most commonly in the personal income tax system. The differences in the taxation of men and women that were noted more commonly provided a tax benefit to women rather than men; for example, in Hungary, a tax allowance is targeted at mothers of more than four children; whereas in Israel, extra tax credit points are available to mothers.

More than half of the countries surveyed (23 countries) indicated that there was a risk of implicit bias in their tax systems, although only 16 countries reported having assessed this. The implicit biases noted by countries were seen to arise from five common gender differences between men and women (Box 1): differences in the level of income between men and women; differences in the nature of income between men and women; the taxpayer unit used in personal income taxation; differences in consumption patterns; and differences in expectations regarding social roles.

As with explicit biases, these implicit biases can occur to the detriment of either gender, depending on how the tax system interacts with these underlying characteristics. For example, the progressivity of the tax system provides a lower tax burden for lower income earners – typically women – while at the same time, producing disincentives in household-based tax systems for second earners to work.

Within both of the explicit and implicit gender bias categories, countries noted examples that either reduced gender bias, or increased it. Based on these different examples, a further disaggregation of the implicit and explicit framework could be considered, as set out in Table 4.1.

Nineteen countries reported using gender budgeting in their country, with five of these countries noting that the gender budgeting framework included specific considerations for tax purposes. Two countries are considering introducing a gender budgeting framework in the near future. Of the countries currently using gender budgeting, the most common basis for this is a high-level political appointment, followed by a specific legislative provision via budget or other law. Three countries reported that this was a constitutional requirement.

Table 4.1. An expanded typology of explicit and implicit bias

	Explicit	**Implicit**
Exacerbate gender bias	Provisions in the tax code, or in formal administration requirements, that explicitly reference gender, and which worsen gender biases present in society. *E.g. lower tax rates for married men; tax credits available for men; women not having access to their tax info.* Policy response: **Remove.**	Tax settings that are gender neutral, but which interact with the different economic and social realities of men and women in ways that worsen gender biases present in society. *E.g. higher tax rates on second earners, informal taxation or user fees on services used more by women, low rates of taxation on capital income or wealth.* Policy response: **Reconsider.**
Reduce gender bias	Provisions in the tax code, or in formal administration requirements, that explicitly reference gender, but which reduce gender biases present in society. *E.g. lower property tax or inheritance rates for women, tax credits for working mothers.* Policy response: **Evaluate.**	Tax settings that are gender neutral, and which interact with the different economic and social realities of men and women in ways that reduce gender biases present in society. *E.g. Improving progressivity of the tax system, reducing disincentives for low income earners to work, broadening tax bases to include capital income.* Policy response: **Promote.**

Source. OECD.

Few countries systematically analyse the impact of tax administration or compliance on gender. The overwhelming majority of countries indicated that they have not designed or implemented analyses on the gender impact of tax administration and compliance measures, nor adjusted their tax administration processes.

Most countries have access to some gender-differentiated data for policy analysis, with 25 of the 43 respondents indicating this. Access to data is concentrated on male and female incomes and the labour market: detailed micro-data on male and female incomes is available in 24 of the 43 countries surveyed and 17 have access to information on male and female labour force participation. Detailed data on consumption (seven countries) and on property and wealth ownership (ten countries) disaggregated by gender is less commonly available.

Finally, countries indicated a number of priorities for future work. The most common preference was for future OECD work to consider the impact of tax credit or tax allowance provisions on gender equity. A secondary priority was the design of explicit tax biases designed to reduce gender inequalities (Figure 3.10). There was also a strong desire for further work to focus on other labour tax issues, with the impact of taxes on second earners, the progressivity of PIT systems, and the impact of tax credits and allowances on gender, among the top four options for future work. A third priority for future work indicated by countries was exploring gender bias in the taxation of capital income and capital (e.g. wealth and inheritance taxes).

Responses to the survey highlight varying degrees of priority and assessment of gender outcomes in tax policy design across the countries surveyed. Key areas where implicit biases were seen to exist in many countries include differences in the nature and level of income, consumption decisions, and the impact of social roles on the outcomes of the tax system. Further analysis could be pursued to improve the awareness of gender biases in country tax systems, in particular implicit ones, with a view to better assess their impact and reduce them as needed. While many countries indicated that gender is taken into account in their tax policy process, this is not a formal requirement in many countries and guidance is rare. A useful step for governments wishing to further address the impact of implicit bias in their tax systems could be to consider guidance on how to take gender into account in tax policy design, as well as for tax administration purposes. Consideration of the impact of changes in the tax structure and mix are also important to assess for their impact on gender outcomes. When available, gender-disaggregated data is useful to understand possible biases and gender-specific patterns. The survey has also highlighted the need to improve data collection on men and women's property and capital ownership, in order to facilitate deeper analysis of these issues, which is one of the priorities for future work.

Annex A. Do you have access to the following gender disaggregated non-tax data available for policy analysis?

Table A.1. Access to gender disaggregated non-tax data available for policy analysis

Response	Detailed micro-data on male and female incomes	Detailed micro-data on male and female consumption	Detailed micro-data on male and female property and wealth ownership	Information on men's and women's participation in businesses (ownership, sectors, employment, senior management)	Information on male and female labour-force participation (hours worked, wages, unemployment, sectoral involvement)	Other gender disaggregated data
Yes	Argentina Australia Belgium Canada Finland France Greece Hungary Iceland Ireland Israel Italy Luxembourg Mexico Netherlands New Zealand Norway San Marino South Africa Spain Sweden United Kingdom United States Uruguay	Argentina Greece Ireland Mexico New Zealand San Marino	Argentina Greece Iceland Ireland Italy Luxembourg Netherlands Norway San Marino United Kingdom	Argentina Australia Canada Finland France Greece Iceland Ireland Mexico Netherlands New Zealand San Marino South Africa Spain Sweden United Kingdom United States Uruguay	Argentina Australia Canada Finland Greece Hungary Ireland Kenya Mexico Netherlands New Zealand Norway San Marino Spain Slovenia South Africa United Kingdom United States	Argentina Australia Belgium Iceland Ireland Israel Italy Mexico Spain
No	Austria Brazil Costa Rica Croatia Germany Portugal Romania Slovenia Tunisia	Austria Brazil Canada Costa Rica Croatia Finland France Germany Hungary Indonesia Israel Kenya Luxembourg	Austria Brazil Canada Costa Rica Croatia France Germany Indonesia Kenya Portugal Romania Slovenia South Africa	Austria Brazil Costa Rica Croatia Germany Romania Slovenia Tunisia	Austria Costa Rica Croatia Germany Indonesia Romania Tunisia	Austria Brazil Costa Rica Croatia Germany Greece Indonesia Peru Romania Slovenia Tunisia

		Portugal Romania Slovenia South Africa Sweden Switzerland Tunisia United States Uruguay	Spain Sweden Switzerland Tunisia United States Uruguay			
Uncertain	Indonesia Kenya Latvia Peru Switzerland	Australia Latvia Italy Netherlands Norway Peru Spain United Kingdom	Australia Hungary Israel Latvia Mexico New Zealand Peru	Hungary Indonesia Israel Italy Kenya Latvia Luxembourg Norway Peru Portugal Switzerland	Brazil Israel Latvia Peru Portugal Switzerland	Canada Finland Kenya Latvia New Zealand Norway South Africa Switzerland United Kingdom

Source: OECD Tax & Gender Stocktaking Questionnaire 2021.

www.ingramcontent.com/pod-product-compliance
Lightning Source LLC
Chambersburg PA
CBHW051235200326
41519CB00025B/7380